INVESTING SUCCESS

How To Conquer **30** Costly Mistakes &
Multiply Your Wealth!

Lynnette Khalfani-Cox

ADVANTAGE WORLD PRESS

Advantage World Press
Published by Advantage World Press
P.O. Box 137
Mountainside, NJ 07092
www.themoneycoach.net

ISBN (10-Digit):1-932450-57-2
ISBN (13-Digit):978-1-932450-57-6
Cataloging in Publication Data Available

Printed in the USA
First Edition (Hardcover) 2005
Reissue (Paperback) 2011

This publication is designed to provide accurate and
authoritative information in regards to the subject matter
covered. It is sold with the understanding the author and
publisher are not engaged in rendering legal, financial or
other professional advice. Laws and practices vary from
state to state and if legal or other expert assistance is
required, the services of a competent professional should be
sought. The author and publisher specifically disclaim any
responsibility for liability, loss or risk that is incurred as a
consequence, direct or indirect, of the use and application
of any of the contents of this book.

FOREWORD

As Lynnette Khalfani so wisely points out, all investors make mistakes from time to time. But the most successful investors are those who are able to learn from these blunders and make wiser decisions in the future.

As someone who has lived and breathed investing for more than 40 years, I can honestly say that many of our most serious mistakes come from our hearts, not our heads. The amazing bull market of the late 1990's created a euphoria that was hard to resist, and an atmosphere that caused a lot of people to ignore time-tested investing basics and throw discipline out the window. Now that we are hopefully witnessing a recovery from the worst bear market since the Depression, it is equally important that investors maintain a cool head and not allow their fears to interfere with thoughtful long-term decisions.

Therefore, I encourage you to take Lynnette's well-researched advice to heart. Set specific, measurable, and realistic goals. Create an asset allocation plan that suits your risk tolerance, time frame, and goals. Buy a diversified mix of investments, being careful not to over concentrate in any one asset class, sector, style, or industry. And perhaps most important of all, make a commitment to being a lifelong investor.

These basics are more important now than ever. They are our investing compass points, and I urge you to take them to heart. I strongly believe that the American stock market is still the best place for long-term investing, and that with a wise investing plan – combined with a cool head -- you can meet your financial goals. I wish you the best.

Charles R. Schwab
Founder and Chairman
The Charles Schwab Corporation
August, 2003

PREFACE

For individual investors there are two sides to the investing equation: first you must know the "right" things to do; second you must avoid doing the "wrong" things. There are hundreds of books that deal with the right way to invest and this topic is subject to a wide diversity of opinions. In this book, Lynnette Khalfani has, to our benefit, decided to concentrate on the second, and equally important, part of the investing equation. She has pointed out what to avoid. And no one is likely to dispute any of the points she so clearly makes on the pages that follow.

The investing world can be a very unfriendly place for the unprepared or under-informed investor. In fact, it can be a veritable minefield for individuals who don't pay attention to their investments or who completely put them under the control of a third party. One misstep can blow apart a lifetime of savings. What Lynnette has done in this book is literally placed large red flags on the investing landscape: showing us the areas to avoid, showing us where the wealth-threatening mines are buried, and marking a pathway through this minefield to the end goal of increased wealth.

As president of an organization devoted to creating investor education material and as a professor of investing studies at the college level, I have personally worked with hundreds of individual investors. In analyzing the activities of those who have performed poorly, it has become apparent that the same mistakes are made over and over again. And even the most savvy of investors makes them. These are the mistakes that are clearly described in this book. Once they are recognized, they can be avoided.

In a clear, concise and easy-to-read manner, Lynnette has detailed the mistakes that prevent investors from attaining the financial goals they really want and are capable of reaching. This is a book you will want to read thoroughly the first time and then scan again each time you review your portfolio of investments; perhaps quarterly, perhaps annually. Avoiding investing mistakes is key to increasing your wealth and therefore this book deserves a place in the library of every individual investor.

Leland B. Hevner
President,
National Association of Online Investors (NAOI)
July 15, 2003

TABLE OF CONTENTS

INTRODUCTION

Have you ever wondered what separates successful investors from marginal ones or from those who get clobbered by Wall Street? The best investors aren't always better stock pickers. Most of them don't boast Ivy-league degrees. Nor do they have access to "inside" information. In truth, the most successful investors – that is, the ones who consistently make money in up and down markets – are simply the people who make the fewest investing mistakes, and those who *quickly* fix the blunders they do make.

Too often, unsuccessful investors think: "If I could just pick the next Microsoft, I'd be rich," or "If only I had sold my stock at its peak, I'd have a fortune." Well, it certainly helps to identify industry-leading companies as potential investments. And "selling high" may bring you one step closer to fattening your bank account. However, the reality is that just buying good investments and selling them for a profit offers absolutely no assurance that you will be a successful investor. In fact, if you *only* master those two elements of buying and selling, you almost certainly will fail miserably as an investor.

THE "BUY LOW, SELL HIGH" MYTH

"Now wait a minute," you may be saying. "Isn't that the very definition of smart investing: knowing *what* to buy and *when* to sell? And what about that old adage: 'buy low and sell high?' Isn't that what this whole investing business is all about?" Actually, nothing could be further from the truth. Here's why:

All the buying and selling savvy in the world won't maximize your wealth if you make any number of costly investing missteps.

Consider, for example: What happens if you trade so much that commissions eat away at your profits? What happens if poor planning or impatience leads you to pay extra taxes to Uncle Sam? What happens if you trust an unscrupulous stockbroker, trustee or accountant, and he skims funds from your account? What happens if your investing strategy fails to take advantage of the benefits of compounded interest?

So sure, you might buy some "winners" for your portfolio — and even sell them at the right time. But what happens if that Wall Street darling you loaded up on nosedives inexplicably right after you purchase it? No bad news from the company. Nothing terrible about its management, product or the industry in which it operates. Just negative overall "market conditions." These are just a fraction of the possible dilemmas that await beginning and long-time investors alike.

MASTERING THE FIVE PHASES OF INVESTING

Despite conventional wisdom, shrewd investing clearly entails far more than buying and selling know-how. Successful investing involves mastering a multi-faceted process, and side stepping the dangers lurking at every turn. These dangers must be avoided to maximize investment performance and multiply your wealth.

By now, you may be asking: "If investing transcends buying and selling, what else is there?"

The investing process involves five distinct phases:
1) Strategizing to meet your personal goals;
2) Buying the right investments;

3) **Holding** and adequately monitoring the investments in your portfolio;

4) **Selling** investments in a judicious manner; and

5) **Dealing effectively** with investment intermediaries such as stockbrokers and financial planners.

Once you recognize the many traps that arise during these five stages, you can readily avoid these perils. And what if you've *already* erred and somehow stepped onto an investing landmine? Don't despair! (You're reading this book, so while you might have "lost your shirt," life and limb remain intact, right?) The key is to better navigate those ticking time bombs going forward.

Remember: you don't have to be perfect. The best investors just make the fewest mistakes, and they readily recover from the fumbles they do commit. The sooner you realize this basic yet powerful truth, the sooner you can begin to turn almost any perilous situation into a profitable one. That is a central message throughout *Investing Success*.

But if you don't remember anything else from *Investing Success*, I would hope that you would remember this most crucial point:

Unsuccessful investors focus on products. They're constantly asking: "What's the best stock to buy?" or "What's the hottest mutual fund?" And if they make poor choices, they are reluctant to properly remedy the situation. By contrast, successful investors focus on the process of investing. They ask: "What should I be doing to grow my portfolio?" or "What strategies will help me reach my goals?" If they err at some point, they are eager to fix their blunders, learn from those miscalculations, and minimize future missteps.

This is a big distinction between unprofitable investors and enormously profitable ones. So, if you find yourself worrying too much about products, you may have to change your mindset to become a successful investor. Also, if you fall into the trap of blaming others for your financial predicament, you may have to re-think things.

As a financial journalist, I realize that corporate scandals, accounting improprieties, and research conflicts of interest have cost the investing public trillions of dollars in recent years. While there is plenty of blame to go around, in the final analysis you are ultimately responsible for your own finances. After all, no one cares about your economic well being more than you do, right? Even if you've lost money on Wall Street in the past due to outside influences, as you read this book I want you to take an honest look in the mirror — and decide whether you also fell victim to your own investing mistakes. It's tough medicine, I know. But I honestly believe that only after you recognize your own mistakes can you remedy them, and start to build true wealth.

THE GENERAL CONCEPT BEHIND *INVESTING SUCCESS*

I hope you didn't pick this book up expecting to be berated for your investing shortcomings (or to give a copy to someone else to berate them for their mistakes!). That's not what this book is about. On the contrary, I want to make it clear that mistakes are a natural – indeed a healthy and very necessary – part of becoming a successful investor. To think that you will completely avoid all investing mistakes is wholly unrealistic. Did you learn to walk without falling down a few times? Of course you didn't. Just as you learned as a toddler to put one sure foot in front of the other, so too will you learn to stroll confidently down this exciting place called Wall Street. Besides, if you didn't make some bad decisions as an investor, I doubt you would really learn what does and does not work, how you should and should not conduct your financial affairs, nor why it's necessary to look at investing as a long-term process, as opposed to a one-shot event.

WHAT DOES A JOURNALIST KNOW ABOUT INVESTING ANYWAY?

I also think it's important to tell you how I came to write *Investing Success*. Some people may ask, and legitimately so, what qualifies me to write an investing book. After all, I'm a financial journalist – not a stockbroker, financial planner or money manager. Well, the truth of the matter is that it's precisely *because* I'm a personal finance journalist that I'm able to share the valuable information you are about to read.

The advice contained in this book isn't Lynnette Khalfani's wisdom (as much as I'd like to claim credit for it). To be sure, I have my opinions and I offer them candidly. But primarily, I've tapped the collective wisdom of hundreds of financial experts and investors just like you. Over the past decade, I've interviewed well over 1,000 financial professionals – from market strategists to hedge fund experts to chief investment officers and so on. When I talked to members of the financial planning community in particular, I noticed patterns in what they would say concerning their clients. Over and over again, people seemed to be making the same types of costly, and largely avoidable, investing errors.

I further saw investors' tendency toward financial mistakes when I began writing a personal finance column for Dow Jones Newswires in 1999. Readers frequently wrote me with investing questions and dilemmas. Later, when I did regular "Financial Fitness" segments on CNBC, the same thing happened. On a weekly basis, viewers would log onto CNBC.com and pose a variety of questions about whatever financial topic I reported on that week. Almost invariably, readers and viewers expressed a higher degree of comfort getting information from me than from their paid advisors. This initially surprised me. I later discovered, though, that these individuals appreciated the fact that I was a neutral third party. I had no investment products to sell, no commissions to earn, no vested interest in their finances.

The same thing is true today. So no, I don't work for a Wall Street brokerage house and I don't have a license to sell securities. Nor is that my intention. If I became such a professional, then I'd probably only give you one person's point of view (my own), or perhaps the bias of my firm. But as a journalist, I'm more than happy to be able to offer you my educated opinion, as well as a wide range of informed ideas from some of the top minds in finance.

HOW TO USE THIS BOOK

Because a winning investment program involves the five crucial areas described above – strategizing, buying, holding/monitoring, selling, and dealing with financial intermediaries – I've organized this book into five easy to understand parts according to those criteria. Furthermore, each chapter is devoted to one investing mistake.

If you are planning your debut plunge into the financial markets, ideally you should read *Investing Success* from cover to cover before spending a dime on any investment. Going through each chapter and each investing mistake sequentially will help you think about investing as a step-by-step process – as opposed to a haphazard series of events that mystify and overwhelm unwitting investors.

Realistically though, you probably won't get your hands on this book before you commit money to an investment. But it doesn't matter if you've just made your first investment or your 500th. What lies between these pages will help you become a more successful investor.

Even if you are a seasoned investor, you too will be best served by reading the text straight through because it will re-focus your thinking, and highlight mistakes you may be making or overlooking. Some highly experienced investors may know what their problem areas are – say, you have difficulty selling investments – and can flip right to those chapters.

There are also several handy symbols used throughout *Investing Success* to guide your reading:

NOTE & REMEMBER: For statistics, facts, resources, and other straight-forward information.

For action items. This is where I give you suggested things to do.

For insights that I want you to think about or visualize, and counter-intuitive points that may cause you to re-consider certain beliefs.

Finally, at the end of each chapter, I offer a "**$ummary $uccess $trategy**". This is the place that succinctly highlights what you should do to avoid or fix the mistake covered in that chapter.

Don't beat yourself up if you find that you're guilty of committing some of the investing faux pas outlined in this book. Countless others – myself included - have made some of the same mistakes. In order to illustrate how widespread investing mistakes are, I have incorporated plenty of first-hand accounts and other information from individual investors with a range of investing know-how from all walks of life. Some of these investors, like famed billionaire Warren Buffett, are legendary and their names are immediately recognizable. One well-known investor is Charles Schwab, founder of Charles Schwab & Co., Inc. During an interview in 2003, he candidly told me "I've made enough investing mistakes to fill *three* books." But *Investing Success* doesn't just capture the know-how of celebrated market professionals.

Other people included in this book you've probably never heard of, but their stories will sound familiar, as they may mirror your own experiences or those of someone you know.

Because investing is such a dynamic process, I hope that even after you close the last pages of *Investing Success*, you will refer back to it whenever you contemplate how to make smarter investment decisions.

Best wishes in your investing endeavors! I know you'll be greatly enriched — and sleep better at night — if you conquer the following 30 investing mistakes.

PART I

STRATEGIC SLIP-UPS

MISTAKE 1

FAILING TO SET SPECIFIC, MEASURABLE, AND REALISTIC GOALS

Do you remember when you were a kid and some adult asked you what you planned to make of yourself in life? That initial conversation probably went something like this:

> **Adult:** Johnny, what do you want to be when you grow up?
>
> **Johnny:** I want to be a fireman.
>
> **Adult:** That's great, Johnny. Why do you want to become a fireman?
>
> **Johnny:** So I can help save people. And also because I want to drive down the street in a big, red fire truck with the sirens going 'Whirr!!! Whirr!!! Whirr!!!'

In the case of my son, who's in pre-kindergarten, his answer is more along the lines of: I want to be a fireman, *and* a baseball player, *and* a teacher, *and* a veterinarian, *and* a (fill-in-the-blank) …

You've got to love kids. They're super-ambitious, and so hopeful about the future. Many of them truly believe that they can achieve anything in life that they want. As adults, especially those of us who are parents, I think we all strive to nurture that natural optimism in children. For young people, having such carefree (translation: unfocused) dreams for the future is a good thing.

However, for adults, particularly those of us who invest, such unbridled optimism can be dangerous. Don't misunderstand me. I'm not saying that you can't have high hopes from a financial standpoint. What I am suggesting, though, is that we can't afford to completely mimic the carefree optimism of children. Youngsters have the luxury of giving little or no thought to the *specifics* of their goals, nor *how* and *when* those aims will be achieved.

WHAT ARE YOUR GOALS?

So many people simply say: "I would like to save more money," or "I want to invest for the future." Well, the first question you really need to answer is: For what *purpose* do you want to save or invest?

We all have personal goals. Some people would like to retire before they turn 60. Others want to build a dream house on the beach. Maybe your ambition is to be able to afford to send your kids to a private college. Or perhaps you're itching to quit your job and form your own company.

All of these personal goals are also financial goals, because it takes money to achieve them. For example, you certainly can't retire in comfort with an empty bank account. Neither can you launch a business without some start-up capital.

Take a few minutes to review the general goals listed below. Do any of them match your own? If so, think about whether each applicable goal is a short, medium, or long-range mission for you.

> **Short-Term goals:** can be achieved in 1-2 years maximum
> **Medium-Term goals**: require 2 -10 years to accomplish
> **Long-Term goals**: require saving/investing for 10+ years

- Pay off credit card debt
- Establish a cash cushion or emergency fund

- Buy a new automobile or a second car
- Retire comfortably
- Make large contribution(s) to church, synagogue, etc.
- Obtain a down payment on a first home
- Fund a family member's college education
- Start a business
- Pay for a wedding
- Pay off student loans
- Return to undergraduate or graduate school
- Take a cruise
- Buy a boat or yacht
- Create a non-profit organization
- Purchase a vacation home
- Travel around the world
- Fund a charitable trust
- Save for a new baby
- Acquire residential or commercial rental property

GOAL-SETTING IS THE FOUNDATION OF SUCCESSFUL INVESTING

Numerous studies show that people who engage in active goal setting – i.e. thinking about their goals *and then writing or typing them out* – overwhelmingly fare better than people who don't set written goals. This is true in investing, and throughout life in general.

There's some science behind this, as well as some common sense. When you write down your goals, and especially when you look at them everyday, they serve as a constant reminder of what you want to achieve. A written mission keeps you focused. It gives you motivation. And perhaps most interestingly, declaring your objectives in black-and-white kicks your subconscious mind into high gear. Without you even trying, your brain starts thinking and strategizing about ways in which you can meet those goals — even while you're sleeping.

Investors who don't bother to define any personal goals lack focus. They buy investments indiscriminately, under the false assumption that simply "being in the market" is somehow beneficial. In reality, such misdirected actions are highly harmful. They frequently result in wasted time, money and energy.

Individuals with hazy or generic goals (like "I want to be rich") are unable to reach them due to an unrealistic or unknown assessment about what it takes to get there. Remember when I said earlier that a lot of people express a general desire to "invest for the future?" Financial planners say that a common refrain among investors is: "I want to have a comfortable retirement."

What exactly does that mean? As you might suspect, it is highly subjective and individualized. For some people, having a "comfortable retirement" may mean making sure their 30-year mortgage is paid off. Others might view free-and-clear ownership of a home as low on the list of priorities. Also, what kind of money are we talking about to achieve "comfort," or *your* preferred quality of life in retirement? Will you require $2,500 or $5,000 monthly, $10,000 or perhaps some other amount? Determining these quality of life preferences are what leads us to the importance of setting the right kinds of goals: so-called SMART goals.

READY, SET, GOAL!

So far, you've figured out *why* you're investing, or why you *want* to invest: It's for retirement, that new boat or the 4,000-square-foot house you want to custom build. Whatever they are, your goals remind you that investing *isn't* about building wealth simply for wealth's sake. Investing should always begin as a goal-oriented process, helping you meet real-life needs and aspirations. As you can tell, goals are personal and values-based.

Still, you'll miss the mark if you stop here. You're far from done in the goal-setting department. Now that you've lumped your goals into short, medium and long-term time tables, you'll want to really hone in on several key points. Namely, you must establish specific, measurable and realistic goals; also known as SMART goals. SMART is an acronym that describes goals that are:

- Specific
- **Measurable**
- Actionable
- **Realistic**
- Time-Bound

Here is an example of a well-crafted SMART goal:

"I want to save $25,000 for a down-payment on a $250,000 4-bedroom, 2 ½ bath colonial home with a pool that I will buy three years from now."

This goal is **specific** – in terms of the dollar amount required, the cost of the house, as well as the type of home desired. It's **measurable**, because you can readily figure out how much you would have to save each year (roughly $8,009 assuming a modest 4% annual return) to come up with the $25,000 down payment. It's **actionable** because no amount of dreaming, wishing, or thinking alone will generate the money. You'll have to *do* something. That could mean making automatic deductions from your paycheck, reducing frivolous spending, or working a second job to meet the goal. Depending on your income, expenses, debts, etc., this may be a stretch goal. But if you earn $50,000 a year or more, this goal is nevertheless realistic. (Even if you don't earn $50,000+, this goal is **realistic** if you are prepared to make financial sacrifices. For instance, do you really need to eat out twice a week for dinner or to get 150 premium-cable channels in your home?). Finally, this goal can keep you on course because it has a definite **time** frame: three years.

SO HOW MUCH WILL THESE GOALS COST?

Ultimately, you will also need to figure out how much money it will take to meet your personal/financial goals. For many short and medium term goals, you probably have a pretty good idea of the costs, so you can just plug in the appropriate numbers. For example, the new car you want retails for $25,000, or you have $10,000 in credit card debt you'd like to get rid of – and sooner rather than later. But what about those far-away goals, like your retirement in 20 years?

There are scores of retirement calculators on the Internet that will quickly tell you, based on a series of assumptions, one of two things:

1. *The amount of money you will have accumulated at retirement* if you make "X" amount of annual contributions;

or

2. *The amount of money you need to save annually* in order to accumulate "X" amount of funds at retirement

To illustrate how these calculators work, let's assume you are 40 years old, you wish to retire at age 65, and that you've already stashed away $50,000 in an Individual Retirement Account or 401(k) plan.

Example 1. If you put away $500 a month for retirement, how much money will you have accumulated at retirement in 25 years? The answer depends on how much you plug in as an expected rate of return. Use a figure between 7% and 10%, depending on how much risk you think you'd be willing to assume. Don't make the mistake of having an impractical (and/or improbable) outlook about your expected investment returns. (In other words, don't assume you'll rack up 25% annual returns. That's an unrealistic projection).

Based on our hypothetical savings of $50,000, and annual contributions of $6,000 ($500 a month times 12 months in a year), you will save $781,059 by retirement. That assumes you will generate 8% returns annually.

Example 2. What if you already know how much you want or need during your golden years? Let's say it's $1,000,000. The next step then is to figure out how much annual savings is necessary to help you reach your $1,000,000 goal. Again, based on the same set of assumptions: you have 25 years to retirement, $50,000 in current savings and you expect your investments will return 8% each year.

In this scenario, to wind up with $1,000,000 upon retirement, you must contribute $8,995 annually (or $750 a month) to your nest egg. Here are a handful of web sites with retirement calculators and useful worksheets that are more comprehensive, yet easy to use:

- www.smartmoney.com
- www.quicken.com
- www.money.cnn.com
- www.kiplinger.com

There are literally tens of thousands of sites out there you can utilize. In early 2003, I did a search on Yahoo! using the key words "retirement calculator." I came up with whopping 206,000 hits!

Many web-based calculators will walk you the through the primary assumptions that a financial planner would in helping you to figure out your expected retirement savings. But be sure to recognize the shortcomings of many calculators and what they can't offer.

- They can't help you figure out how much you can realistically afford to set aside given all your current obligations (mortgage/rent, car payments, credit card debt, utility bills, not to mention basics like food and transportation).

- Also, while most calculators take inflation into account, others don't.

- Some web sites offer general guidance about how your expenses in retirement may rise (such as higher travel and medical expenses) or fall (no more commuting costs or buying suits for the office). But others make no mention of that.

- Moreover, some retirement calculators fail to consider at all the impact of other money you may have coming. Besides your savings, your post-retirement income can be derived from sources such as Social Security benefits, trusts, annuities, pensions or an expected inheritance.

HOW A FINANCIAL PLANNER CAN HELP

This is where having a good financial planner can be of value. He or she won't just calculate the specific dollar amounts it will take to fund each of your goals. Based on a careful, tailored assessment of your personal situation – your individual risk tolerance, your health, the amount of money you have already saved, the funds you can continue to save regularly, and any other relevant information – that advisor can offer feedback on everything from how feasible your goals are to how you can best prioritize them.

Furthermore, after reviewing your entire portfolio, and evaluating the securities in which you'll be investing, an advisor can use historical investment averages as a benchmark for setting your targeted investing returns. If you get good service and an advisor who will act as your "financial quarterback," the fees you pay will probably be well worth it, especially if you are a procrastinator and the advisor can get you going with a workable financial plan.

Let's assume for now, however, that you're flying solo. (At least, you are while you're reading this book). Here's where your work begins.

Based on what you've just learned, **write out your top five personal goals**.

If you're feeling especially ambitious, list 10 of them. Note whether they are short-term, medium or long-range targets. Also, be sure to make them SMART goals; nothing generic or pie-in-the-sky.

_____

_____

_____

_____

_____

_____

_____

_____

_____

At this stage, if you've actually taken the time to *write down* your goals (and I hope that you have!) you're ahead of 90% of the pack. Many people *think about* and *say* they want this or that goal. But relatively few individuals take the time to commit their words and goals to paper. For investors, that's a big mistake.

You *must* have detailed, written goals in order to direct your plan of action. Otherwise, you're not investing wisely. You're really just dreaming of getting rich.

And again, there's nothing wrong with dreaming per se. It's just that you've got to ground those dreams in reality. After all, you're not a kid anymore. You're a grown-up, right?

$UMMARY $UCCESS $TRATEGY
TO CONQUER INVESTING MISTAKE #1:

Set specific, measurable and realistic goals. Write out your unique dreams, such as saving a certain amount for your child's college tuition or retirement by a certain age. Goals help you remember that investing is done for a purpose.

2

MISTAKE

INVESTING PREMATURELY

This chapter is probably going to "tick off" a lot of people in the brokerage industry. It may make a lot of you investors angry too – at least at first. Nevertheless, there is something that millions of investors need to know. And since your stockbroker probably won't tell you this, I will:

Many of you have absolutely no business being in the stock or bond markets right now.

That's right, I said you shouldn't be currently investing. Why on earth would I say that? Especially in a book that's telling you about investing. Simply put, a lot of you don't yet have your financial house in order. And investing at this stage is investing prematurely, probably to your long-term detriment.

Allow me to explain myself here.

As a financial journalist over the past decade, I've interviewed hundreds of people who have lost money in the financial markets. Some losses were relatively small. In other cases, the losses amounted to tens or hundreds of thousands of dollars. Needless to say, the financial hit these investors took hurt.

FINANCIAL WORRIES RUN DEEP

But there is another, less obvious – and often overlooked – cause behind these investors' dismay. A big reason investors have so much angst over their mistakes and losses in the financial markets is because they're also anxiety-ridden over their general lack of financial security.

Surveys consistently show that each New Year's holiday, one of the top resolutions for Americans (besides losing weight) is getting their personal finances in order. By and large, the average American's finances are in shambles – and most people know it, even if they don't quite know why they have financial problems.

To compound the situation, some investors (consciously or not) are mistakenly counting on their investments to "fix" a whole lot of things that have long been neglected in their lives: things like planning for their family's future and getting their debt under control. These investors erroneously think that as long as their portfolios keep growing, they'll somehow be financially prepared to handle any circumstance. So when that quarterly statement arrives in the mail, showing that they've lost money, these investors get panicky. Deep down they fear that their investments have gone awry – just like the rest of their financial lives.

While many of these individuals were busy reading the *Wall Street Journal*, analyzing stock charts, or pouring over mutual fund data, what they should've been doing is putting their energies into taking care of the basics of their personal finances.

I can sum up the financial basics in two words: Will DIED. Or maybe it's better put this way:

Will   Will and Testament
D   Debt
I   Insurance
E   Emergency Stash
D   Disability

GET A WILL WHILE YOU'VE GOT A LIFE

At some point, all of us will die. It's an obvious fact of life. But it's also a reality that most of us don't like to think about, much less *talk* about, or *act* on.

Remember September 11, 2001? Of course you do. Who can forget the attacks on the World Trade Center in New York, the Pentagon in Washington D.C. and the airplane passengers who overtook their hijackers before crashing in the mountains in Pennsylvania?

Of the thousands of people who died on Sept. 11th, many of them were young men and women in their 30s and 40s. Most left behind young children, spouses, or other loved ones. Unfortunately, what many of them *didn't* leave behind was a will: a simple legal document expressing their wishes and how they would like their personal and financial affairs to be handled upon their demise.

> Unfortunately, in today's world, people die prematurely from all kinds of dangers, accidents, diseases and other causes. That's one reason why having a will is critical.

HERE'S WHAT A WILL CAN DO:

- Provide for your loved ones by letting you determine when and what assets should go to various family members, friends or charities

- Allow you to designate a guardian to care for your minor children
- Avoid the time and expense of an unnecessarily lengthy probate. (A will must be probated, or proved valid by a court. With a well-prepared will, your estate can be settled much more quickly)
- Minimize the chances of family squabbling after your death, because you've clearly expressed your wishes
- Reduce the emotional turmoil your loved ones will experience, since at least there is a plan laid out

Despite these advantages, it's estimated that more than 70% of all Americans don't have a will. And yes, yes, yes, I know you're busy. Join the club. We've all got too much to do and not enough time to squeeze in everything. But answer this question: what is your priority? Is it handling your financial affairs or watching television? According to Nielsen Media Research, the average adult in the U.S. spends more than 4 hours a day watching television. Can you turn off the TV for just one week? No sports, news, soap operas or dramas. Spend that time instead thinking about and acting upon how to best leave your personal affairs.

When you do die, you'll be doing the people you leave behind a big favor if you've prepared your will. In the event of your death, they'll already have to deal with a big emotional blow. Don't compound their grief by burdening them with unnecessary worries over things like: Who would Sarah have wanted to take care of the kids? Or why didn't Dennis leave a will?

EXCESSIVE DEBT: THE ULTIMATE FINANCIAL DOOM

How much credit card debt are you carrying right now? Less than a thousand bucks? More than $3,000? Have you hit the $10,000 mark?

Take a look at the following statistics. They help explain why many people think Americans are in the midst of a credit-card frenzy.

The Debt Toll Rises ...

- The typical U.S. household has 13 cards, including bank, retail and debit cards
- The average credit card debt for those with a balance totals $8,940
- The average annual interest rate on credit cards issued nationwide is 14.7%

Source: Cardweb.com

Here are the two sides to this issue. On the one hand, critics say the credit card industry has kicked its marketing machine into massive overdrive when it comes to offering credit cards to consumers.

> According to the Consumer Federation of America (CFA), credit card issuers mail five billion solicitations annually. That works out to roughly 50 per U.S. household, which explains why you probably get at least one credit card offer each week.

"Credit card issuers are shamelessly escalating their marketing and available credit to stratospheric levels," says Travis Plunkett, CFA Legislative Director.

On the other hand, the credit card industry says it is simply making credit available to a public that desires to do everything from buying clothes, to renting automobiles and booking hotel rooms.

A WAY OUT OF DEBT

Here's my position: For better or worse, Americans have an unprecedented amount of debt. Only you know if your personal level of debt is a burden to you. If that is the case, then it's time you acted to do something about it.

> If you're an investor carrying more debt than is comfortable, you may have wondered whether it is more prudent to invest first or pay off your credit card bills first. In most cases, the answer is a no-brainer: pay those credit card bills first.

A simple example illustrates why. Assume you have a $3,000 balance on your Visa card, which is costing you 14.7% in annual interest. And let's say you came into $3,000 – maybe a job bonus or a refund check from the IRS. Well, if you wanted to invest that money in the financial markets, you'd have to rack up a 14.7% return (after taxes) to match the effective return you could get from paying off your Visa credit card. Can you (or anyone else for that matter) *guarantee* a 14.7% return if you invest? Absolutely not. So if you're really serious about investing or wanting to invest (and I trust that you are since you've picked up this book), do yourself a favor and get that credit card debt in check first.

I know some of you are thinking one of two things:

1) If I wait until I pay off all my credit-card debt, it could take years!

or

2) I'm *already* investing, via my 401(k), IRA, or mutual funds, and there's NO WAY I'm going to stop investing until I pay off those blasted credit card bills!

In both cases, don't worry. In the second half of this chapter, I'm going to tell you how you can best handle your debt *in less than 30 days* – no matter what your situation. If you follow my advice, you'll be prepared to invest – and you won't make the mistake of investing prematurely.

INSURANCE

Let us revisit the issue of the Sept. 11th victims. Many of those killed worked on Wall Street. They were stockbrokers, traders, analysts, and so on. The irony is that these Wall Street professionals spent a huge amount of time and effort trying to make money – for others and themselves. Yet, lots of them neglected to make the one sure bet that would have brought financial security to their loved ones. By doing one simple thing, buying life insurance, in addition to playing the stock market, they could've provided far more long-term protection for their family members.

Learn a lesson from that tragedy: purchase life insurance coverage right away to provide for your family in the event of your death. Obtain a policy that would give your beneficiaries a payout that is at least five to seven times your annual salary. Depending on your personal situation, more may be advisable. (For example, if you have young children, you may want to make sure their college educations are paid for in the event of your death). Remember, life insurance isn't an investment per se. It's designed to replace your income and give financial stability to your family in your absence.

WHEN DOES $500 RESULT IN A $1,000,000 PAYOFF?

Before you say you can't afford to buy life insurance, realize this: for a healthy 40-year-old man who is a non-smoker, a 20-year term life insurance policy with a $1,000,000 benefit is well under $1,000, with policies in the $500 to $700 range being the most common. Isn't that kind of protection worth it? Therefore, take a fraction of the money you're committing to stocks or mutual funds and buy a good life insurance policy. Later on in this chapter, I'll tell you where you can find the right kind of life insurance policy at a cost you can afford.

EMERGENCY STASH

Did you know that in May 2003, some nine million people in the U.S. were unemployed? The national unemployment rate also rose to 6.1% - the highest jobless level since July 1994, according to the Labor Department. Anyone who has ever been downsized knows the stress and the financial challenges that a layoff can bring. If you've never been through a layoff, count yourself fortunate. But don't be fooled into thinking that it couldn't happen to you simply because your boss really likes you or your job performance has been excellent.

Indulge me a moment here. Assume your boss came to you and said: "I'm sorry, but the economy is weak, our company's having hard times, and unfortunately, we're going to have to eliminate your position." What would you do? (I mean after you picked up your jaw).

How long would you be able to pay your mortgage or rent? Would you be able to keep up with those credit card payments … without having to use one card to pay off another? Think about all the luxuries you currently enjoy. How soon would you have to fire the gardener, eliminate trips to the hair or nail salon, forego restaurant dinners, or cut back on renting videos each weekend? If you've been investing, would you have to sell some of your investments to pay for your monthly living expenses? If so, that would lead to a nasty tax hit.

SET ASIDE THREE TO SIX MONTHS EXPENSES

To avoid cramping your current lifestyle and to minimize your stress in the event of a financial emergency, it's vitally important that you work towards building a three-to-six month cash cushion. This means that if your monthly expenses are $3,000, you should have an emergency stash of at least $9,000. A cushion of $18,000 is far better. Does saving three to six months of your expenses seem like a pipe dream that will take forever? If you continue reading the remainder of this chapter, I'll show you some smart ways you can very quickly get the emergency cushion you need – and prepare to invest wisely. Alternatively, you can make accumulating your cash cushion one of your short or medium range financial goals.

DISABILITY PROTECTION

I've already explained why you need life insurance – it's to provide for your family members after your death. But life insurance alone doesn't adequately protect your family. What if you somehow get injured? The fact is that your chances of being disabled during your working years is four to five times greater than your chances of dying during the same time period. In fact, in any given year, one out of 10 people will become seriously disabled.

Let's hope you're not one of those individuals whose badly injured in a car accident or some other such mishap and is unable to go to work. You don't want a disability to cost you your house, your lifestyle, or your savings and investments. The answer? Get a disability insurance policy as quickly as possible.

QUICK-FIX SOLUTIONS TO GET YOUR FINANCIAL HOUSE IN ORDER – AND PREPARE YOU TO INVEST

If you've been reading this chapter closely, you probably realize that I'm not saying you have to be 100% debt free, have a million dollar life insurance policy, purchase expensive disability coverage, etc. before you start to invest, or continue to invest your money. Instead, I'm simply saying take care of the basics. Get some kind of life insurance. Protect your income stream as best you can. Do a bit of financial planning before you venture into stocks, bonds, mutual funds and other investments.

Here's how anyone can quickly put their financial house in order – or at least patch it up sufficiently in order to invest with a much higher degree of financial security.

GET THE WILL TO DRAW UP A WILL

This is one area where you can't afford to procrastinate. To create a will, you basically have two options: retain a professional or do it on your own.

Option 1.
Call a lawyer, make an appointment to see him/her as soon as possible and get a will drafted immediately. Make that call today. Your family is depending on you.

Option 2.
If you're more of a do-it-yourselfer, or if you can't afford to hire an attorney, I recommend using a good software program that will walk you, step by step, through the process of creating your own will. These are a few helpful websites to aid you in this endeavor:

- www.nolo.com
- www.ezlegal.com
- www.standardlegalsoftware.com
- www.legalzoom.com

If you use a software program, I'd still recommend having an attorney who specializes in wills give your document a once-over. This review will be much cheaper than hiring the lawyer to actually create the will. But getting that feedback will give you peace of mind and the assurance that everything is done properly, as required by the laws in your particular state.

One caveat to all you procrastinators out there: Please don't do what I did. My husband and I prepared our wills– and then we took seven months to get the darned things notarized! The wills just sat up at our house, lacking witness signatures and a notary public's seal. Without these crucial final touches, our wills were invalid.

SLAY THE DEBT DRAGON

Here's how you can conquer your debt dilemma, and get ready to invest with the least amount of financial worry:

- If you've got the money, for goodness sakes go ahead and pay off at least some portion of your credit card debt. (I'm amazed at the number of financial planners who tell me that their clients have plenty of money sitting in the bank, but nevertheless have many thousands of dollars in high-interest credit card debt).

- What if you're cash poor but house rich? Then seriously consider taking out a home equity loan to convert your credit card and consumer debt into mortgage debt. (All that interest you're paying on charge cards, student loans, and/or automobiles is not tax deductible. But you can write off up to $100,000 annually in interest on mortgage debt, including a home equity loan).

- If you're short on cash, don't own a home or haven't got equity in your house, immediately call your credit card companies and ask for a lower interest rate. If you've been paying on time, you'd be surprised at how readily they will agree to a rate reduction. (They don't want to lose your business to the competition).

- If you find yourself able to only make minimum payments, cut up your credit cards or at least stop carrying them with you. Eliminate all future credit card spending for which you can't pay off the entire balance by the time the bill arrives.

- For those drowning in debt, and in need of expert help, consult a debt-counseling agency. Two reputable resources are *www.debtreliefclearinghouse.com* and *www.debtadvice.org.*

- Bottom line: Establish a realistic plan for aggressively paying off your debt. *As long as you stick with it,* **you won't be harming yourself by simultaneously investing and reducing your debt load.**

INVESTIGATE INSURANCE OPTIONS

- Find out if you have life insurance coverage from your employer. Verify the exact amount of your benefits. Companies that offer this perk typically give your heirs a lump sum payout based on your annual salary.

- Go see your human resources specialist or employee benefits administrator as soon as possible. Ask about whether you can increase your coverage on the job. Often, you can double your life insurance benefit amount – say, from 1 ½ times your salary to three times your salary – for a very modest deduction from your paycheck.

- Read up on the two kinds of life insurance: permanent and term. For most people, term is the best option and the most affordable. Go on the Internet to learn more about each. Then head to these web sites to comparison shop for the best available policies:

- www.insurance.com
- www.selectquote.com
- www.insure.com
- www.quickquote.com
- www.insweb.com

5 WAYS TO ESTABLISH AN EMERGENCY STASH

We've all heard it said that you should "save for a rainy day." Well, try telling that to someone who's barely able to pay all their *current* obligations, including utility bills, credit cards, car loans, housing, and so forth.

I know it can be a hardship to put money aside to prepare for the unexpected. For years, my husband and I struggled to do it. But now we save every month – automatically. And so can you. You can build your emergency stash little by little if you make your savings systematic, and if you truly commit to saving each and every month — no matter whether the roof starts leaking or the transmission goes out on your car.

Would you like to jump-start your plans to accumulate a cash cushion? Here are five easy ways:

1. **Sell stuff you don't need.** A yard sale featuring your unwanted electronics, clothing, furniture, household goods, computer equipment, art, etc. could net you a tidy sum to start your emergency fund.
2. **Cut out unnecessary spending.** Dispense with magazine subscriptions, cable television, daily lattes from Starbucks, etc. Divert the money you save into your emergency fund each month. **Shopaholics:** see my advice on page 40A.

3. **Slash your current monthly expenditures**. Most people pay more than they should for everything from long-distance telephone service to car leases simply because they don't take the time to shop around, according to Matt Coffin, CEO of Lowermybills.com. To see where you can cut your expenses, log onto *www.lowermybills.com*. Also log onto *www.capitaloneautofinance.com* to find out how to lower your monthly car payment by refinancing your auto loan.

4. **Get a second job** – even if only temporarily. Commit the extra funds solely to your emergency stash. Above all: make your savings automatic by having a fixed amount of funds transferred regularly from your paycheck(s) into your emergency fund. If you don't get the money in your hands, you're less likely to spend it. And chances are you won't miss it either.

5. **Secure a line of credit.** To develop an instant three to six month emergency reserve, obtain a personal line of credit. Rates vary from 6% to 14% depending on your credit history and the size of the credit line you establish. A better option for homeowners is to get a tax-deductible home equity line of credit. Most are currently under 6%. But caution: **Don't use the credit line for any reason other than a legitimate emergency.** The point is to have this credit line as your stand-by while you build up your personal savings. Having a credit line is also a good hedge against a job loss. If you ever get terminated, you already have the credit line at your disposal. But trying getting a credit line when you've lost your job, which is exactly when you'd need it, right? Well, be forewarned: Without a job, the bank loan officer will probably laugh you right out the door.

DISABILITY

Again, see the web sites listed above for insurance quotes. Additionally, look for these features in a disability policy:

- **Annual Inflation Rider** (Find a policy that pays additional benefits as the cost of living index rises)
- **Non-cancelability** (Get a policy that can't be canceled up to age 65, with the option to renew if you keep working)
- **Waiting period** (A one-to-six month period before your benefits begin is common. For the lowest priced coverage, pick the longest waiting period you think you could manage without financial aid, preferably 90 days or more for the best rates)
- **Definition of disability** (Select a policy that defines disability as an inability to work at your regular occupation)

If you are an individual who will diligently follow the advice in this chapter, congratulations. You're on the pathway to becoming a successful investor. You won't make the mistake that so many others do of investing before they're truly ready.

If you're a stockbroker or financial advisor, it may seem like heresy to turn away a client's money and tell that individual to first clean up his financial house. But think about it this way: When investment losses occur – and inevitably, they *will* occur – which client is more likely to phone your office completely stressed over the market, totally irate and practically demanding your head on a platter?

Client A: Whose investment portfolio just went down 10%, but she is debt-free, has a six-month cash cushion, adequate life insurance and disability coverage, as well as a carefully crafted will?

Or

Client B: Whose portfolio also went down 10%, but is struggling to make his credit card payments, has no savings to speak of, and lacks life insurance, disability protection and a written will?

You decide.

$UMMARY $UCCESS $TRATEGY

TO CONQUER INVESTING MISTAKE #2:

Handle some financial basics before investing. Pay down credit card debt, if you can. Draw up a will, get life and disability insurance coverage, and set aside a cash cushion of three to six months' expenses in case of an emergency.

THE SECRETS TO SHOPPING WELL AND LOOKING LIKE A MILLION BUCKS
(Without Spending A Small Fortune)

OK, so this part of the chapter is for all you serious shopaholics out there – gals and guys! But ladies, this information is particularly valuable to you if:

- You'd like to get your shopping habit under control; or
- You want to *look* like a million bucks – without having to actually *spend* that much.

For most of you, I'm guessing that you have plenty of bills to pay, not enough cash to go around, and you've made countless broken New Year's resolutions about managing your money more wisely. If this sounds like you, then *now is the perfect time* to get your act together! To save yourself big bucks, remember my Top 10 Rules for Money-Wise Shoppers. These are strategies that every true fashion aficionado knows (but will never tell):

1. NEVER PAY FULL RETAIL PRICE. EVER.

I'm not suggesting that you walk into Barneys, or even your local department store, and start haggling over prices. But any savvy fashion editor or stylist will tell you that nobody (in the know) pays the full asking price for anything these days.

Here are a few pointers:

- For starters, you can *wait until the item goes on sale* (trust me, it will!)
- *Shop sample sales* in major cities and get designer duds for a fraction of the retail price. These to-die-for sales usually happen after Fashion Week in New York, Los Angeles, London, Milan and Paris.
- *Buy classic styles off-season*. Great pieces look good season to season.
- *Hop online*. All of the following web sites sell designer merchandise both in and off-season: decadestwo.com (for vintage chic); yoox.com (for Italian designers); bluefly.com;

ebay.com (yes, ebay! It offers high-end designer clothes, including some that hit the Net before they're available nationally); overstock.com; and starwares.com (for celebrity duds).

- *Think Outlets, Outlets, Outlets.* The book *Buying Retail Is Stupid! The National Discount Guide to Buying Everything at up to 80% Off Retail,* written by Trisha King and Deborah Newmark, offers state-by-state listings of factory outlets. Last time I checked, this comprehensive, 396-page guide, could be bought on Amazon.com for just $2.55.

- Finally, *you can actually negotiate* in many boutiques and specialty stores. Don't be obnoxious about it. But when you find something you want, just sort of wrinkle your nose up a bit and, while holding the price tag, ever-so-nicely ask the sales person: "$75? Is that the best price you can offer me?"

2. DON'T SHOP ANOTHER DAY UNTIL YOU *ORGANIZE YOUR CLOSET FIRST.*

In your head, you may think you *need* another black skirt. But you probably just *want* one, because if you carefully go through your closet (that's right, sort out all those folded piles and even the stuff in bags and tucked away in the corners), you'll probably find that you have at least two or three – and likely even more – perfectly fine black skirts. So it's hard to justify buying yet another black skirt under these circumstances. By organizing your closet, you'll also be far less prone to making impulse purchases of other things you mistakenly believe you "need."

3. THINK LIKE A CELEBRITY.

When you see Halle Berry or Jennifer Lopez donning a gorgeous dress, wearing Harry Winston jewels, or even sporting a sexy pair of Jimmy Choo shoes, *realize that they rarely ever pay for clothes and accessories.* In fact, designers shower them with goods knowing that having these A-list celebrities wear their clothes will be good publicity and thus boost sales. The celebs themselves more often than not will wear the item once (if the designer is lucky).

But then that item gets donated to charity or tossed in the back of what I'm sure is the world's largest walk-in closet. In any event, consider this: Since multi-millionaire "superstars" aren't even paying to look like stars, why should you? If you keep in mind that a $1,000 dress you're pining away for is probably only realistically going to be worn by you just once (like the stars do), chances are you may be willing to forego splurging on that item if you can't really afford it.

Manolos And Mutual Funds

I'm not suggesting that you can't ever splurge. It's just that you have to be wise about it, and willing to exercise *some* restraint. So while you're *thinking* like your favorite celebrity, don't feel that you can't sometimes *dress* the part as well. After all, most of us would love to have a closet full of shoes like "Sex in the City's" Carrie Bradshaw, right? Well, you really don't have to choose between Manolos and mutual funds. Smart women can – and often do – have both. I know some of you may be thinking: "A pair of Manolo Blahnik shoes can cost upwards of $500. I don't have that kind of cash. But I really want them, so I'll just charge them." But please don't fall into the "debt trap." To get the red carpet looks that Hollywood actresses and New York models flaunt, find the best consignment store in the ritziest neighborhood you know. Go there and "recycle" your wares for cash. Use the money for mutual funds or, if you simply can't resist, those killer Manolos. With a little creative thinking and a willingness to splurge only occasionally, it is possible to keep that New Year's resolution about getting your finances together – without having to say goodbye to fashion.

4. TAKE A FRIEND SHOPPING.

And I don't mean your girlfriend whose Visa bill is constantly more than her rent. I'm talking about your level headed friend; the one who doesn't call you every other week to borrow money because her paycheck has run out. One suggestion though: don't drag along a pal (however well-intentioned) who simply can't have fun on your shopping quest. Instead, bring along your "I-know-how-to-enjoy-myself-too-but-I'm-not-going-to-squander my-rent-payment-to-do-it" buddy. What's the point of all this? A friend with a good head on her shoulders will keep you from making outlandish purchases and wasting your money. She'll make you accountable for your spending actions. And accountability counts.

5. ESTABLISH A PRE-SET LIMIT BEFORE YOU GO SHOPPING.
Just come up with a ballpark figure (say $500) and let that serve as your cap. Now here's where you get to *really* enjoy yourself – and not feel deprived. Mentally allow yourself the option of going 10% over your pre-set limit. So if you absolutely can't do without $50 worth of lingerie, but you've already reached your $500 limit, you can go ahead and make the purchase, and do so guilt-free. Any spending beyond that, though, and you're asking for trouble. This way, if you stick to your pre-set limit, you'll be patting yourself on the back. If you go as high as your spending-cap-plus-10%-limit, at least you've still stayed within the guidelines, without breaking the bank. Bonus: if you actually spend 10% under your limit, celebrate! One caveat: don't spend the 10% you saved (and then some) on an expensive dinner or some other one-time event. Instead, sock that money away into a "hands-off" savings account.

6. GO WHERE THE REAL BARGAINS ARE.
Serious fashionistas who can swing it go to London or Milan for fashion bargains. The cost of the airplane ticket can be well worth it if you pick up, say, Italian boots for $100 that you'd spend $450 for in the U.S. You'd obviously only use this strategy when you're planning to buy multiple items for which the savings alone would pay for the cost of your travel.

7. FREQUENT DISCOUNT RETAILERS.
Pick up the trendiest looks at stores like Target and H&M. Don't worry that the clothes didn't come from a so-called upscale retailer. Most times, no one will know the difference.

8. MAKE MENTAL COMPARISONS.

When you are tempted to plop down a big chunk of money for, say, a cashmere sweater (and yes, I know it's a beautiful one), ask yourself: is this *really* worth a full day's pay? For more expensive items, think: is this truly worth a week (or whatever time) of my labor?

9. DO SOMETHING RADICAL.

If you find yourself at the mall every week (or even every day), plan to make a radical change – if only temporarily. Make a vow to do ABSOLUTELY NO SHOPPING whatsoever for an entire month, or for whatever period of time you think you can stand it. You'd be surprised how much strength you can muster up if you put your mind to it. And while you're saving gobs of money in the process, you'll find other creative uses of your time – and cash.

10. GIVE AWAY SOMETHING.

Emulate your favorite celebrity and make a donation to a worthwhile cause. Surely you have something in the back of your closet, or packed away in the attic or basement, that you've not worn in a month of Sundays. Give it to a charity or a woman's shelter. There's truth in the saying: "What goes around, comes around." You give something to someone else in need, and your generosity will come back to you in some way. In other words: to get a blessing, first *be* a blessing!

INVESTING SUCCESS

3

OPERATING WITHOUT A PRUDENT
ASSET ALLOCATION STRATEGY

If you set about to take a cross-country driving trip, chances are you would consider a map a "must have" item. Well, just as you'd no sooner drive from New Mexico to Maine without a roadmap, you also shouldn't put your investing program into high gear without the benefit of having an exact set of directions as to where you're going. Nevertheless, that's exactly what millions of investors do everyday when they invest without a clearly defined asset allocation strategy.

Recall briefly the investment goals I discussed in Chapter 1 of this book. Reflect especially on your own written goals. Those goals represent your final destination – or where you want to go. Your asset allocation strategy is the roadmap that guides you there.

After you take into consideration your current age, investment time-horizon, your ability to stomach risk, and your goals, you need to get down to the business of dividing fixed percentages of your money to stocks, bonds, and cash (and possibly other investments). That's what asset-allocation is. The idea is to build a portfolio where you establish target percentages (or percentage ranges) and invest money accordingly in differing asset classes. One big benefit to doing this is that you systematically diversify your investment holdings.

Over the past several decades, numerous hypothetical investment models have suggested the following recommended allocations, based on a person's age, risk appetite, and so on:

- Very aggressive portfolio: 100% stock funds
- Moderately aggressive portfolio: 70% stocks; 20% bonds; and 10% cash
- Moderate portfolio: 50% stocks; 35% bonds; 15% cash
- Conservative portfolio: 30% stocks; 50% bonds; 20% cash

But you should know that any formal statistical model is only as good as the specific assumptions that underlie it. Essentially, the makers of the models, and users of it, are assuming that certain investment trends will continue. The thinking goes something like this: "Well, historically, we know that stocks have returned roughly 10% over a 10-year cycle, fixed income investments have returned 6%, and so on."

Of course, statistical models are derived based on what happened in the past. No one can predict the future — so don't waste your time and money calling a psychic hotline to ask where the Dow will be next January! Still, asset allocation helps anchor your investing program. It's the right way – indeed it's the only sane way - to guide you through the investing process. Most accomplished investors will tell you in a heartbeat that it's impossible to pick winners and avoid losers year and year out. If you too want to become a savvy investor, take some time to craft an asset allocation plan.

Imagine that you are lost in a dark tunnel. Your only way out is with a flashlight. And in the midst of hearing bats, rats, and who knows what around you, you're thankful that your flashlight's batteries are working well. That flashlight is illuminating just enough of the tunnel ahead for you to walk through fairly confidently. Just as you have an end goal in sight for which you are investing (retirement, perhaps?), so too you have an objective here. Your goal is to make it safely to the tunnel's exit point. As you carefully make your way through the tunnel, you won't see every little jagged rock on the ground or every red ant crawling about that could potentially bite you. And truth be told, you don't need to see all those dangers. By and large, though, you will be able to make out the huge boulders to dodge, the big puddles of water you should walk around, and the walls that you must avoid running into. That flashlight will be critical to getting you to the light of day. As an investor, so will your asset allocation plan.

Having a well-prescribed asset allocation plan is crucial for several reasons. For starters, with a proper asset allocation plan, you will be less inclined to buy and sell based on emotions. An asset allocation plan also imposes discipline and consistency to your investing efforts. Additionally, an asset allocation plan reduces risk, since no investment category performs well all the time. And with a proper asset allocation strategy, when one category is faring poorly (say small cap growth stocks are out of favor), chances are another category you've also invested in (like large cap value stocks) are performing well.

This brings me to perhaps the single biggest argument in favor of asset allocation. Research shows that 90% of portfolio performance is determined by asset allocation. Take a minute and think about what that statement means.

It really boils down to this: In the final analysis, your ability to multiply your wealth by investing is not based on what individual stocks or bonds you buy. It's not governed by whether or not you have a high-priced fund manager. It's not dictated by whether you pour money into one sector versus another. Making money investing is chiefly determined by how well you divide up your money into different types of assets.

ASSET ALLOCATION GONE AWRY

Denis Walsh, president of Money Concepts, says one of the biggest mistakes he sees is people "buying investments that are far riskier than they realize." Walsh recalls, for instance, the height of the mania during the dot-com era. "I remember when we did asset allocation strategy for clients and they got angry because we didn't have enough in technology," he says, adding that some really irate clients left the firm.

No doubt those same clients were kicking themselves later when the tech meltdown occurred beginning in March 2000. Clearly, the absence of an asset allocation strategy leads to investors buying inappropriate investments, having portfolios that are improperly diversified, and under-performing the broader market.

DON'T FORGET REAL ESTATE

As you contemplate the best asset allocation for your individual needs, don't just think stocks, bonds and cash. If you have substantial assets to invest (roughly $250,000 to $500,000 or more), you'd be wise to also consider "alternative investments" such as gold, energy or other commodities. Even with far less money, many investors would be well served by diversifying with real estate. For those who want broad exposure to the real estate market, REITS, or real estate investment trusts are the best way to go.

Housing prices have skyrocketed in recent years and historically low interest rates have led millions of people to purchase their first homes or trade up to bigger ones. New home construction also remained strong in 2003, all of which led economists, Wall Street pundits, and others to debate whether or not a "bubble" existed in the housing market. If so, that "bubble" did little to dampen the performance of REITS, many of which continued to yield anywhere from 5% to 9%, thanks mostly to the hefty dividends they pay.

Perhaps best of all, REITS let you enjoy the benefits of owning residential or commercial property "without the hassles of being a landlord" says Leo Wells, head of the Wells Real Estate Investment Trust in Atlanta, and one of the best known and most widely-respected experts in the industry.

SOME SIMPLE RULES DON'T WORK

If you're unsure as to whether your portfolio should be aggressive, moderate or conservative (or some variation thereof), it will be money well spent to have a consultation with an investment advisor who can walk you through the process of determining what's right for you. You can also visit the plethora of investing web sites that allow you to take "money personality" tests and so on. These sites often also feature specific areas designed to assess your risk tolerance and asset allocation needs. That will give you some big-picture guidance.

What you shouldn't make the mistake of doing is using someone else's asset allocation strategy. What's best for your sister-in-law or your Uncle Tony isn't likely to be most appropriate for you.

You also shouldn't take this important strategic step and boil it down to an over-simplified method. Yet, that's what many investors have been told to do for years. They were advised to use the "Rule of 100."

For a multitude of reasons, I think you'd be smart to largely disregard the "Rule of 100." This outmoded rule asserts that people should subtract their age from 100 and use the final number as the percentage of assets to invest in stocks. Thus, a 40-year-old man using the Rule of 100 would invest 60% of his assets in stocks. The remaining 40% would be allocated to bonds and cash.

Here's why the rule of 100 doesn't make sense anymore (if it ever did). People are living longer than ever. Advances in healthcare and medicine, and improvements in technology mean that a person who is now age 65 can probably count on seeing age 85. Moreover, the 80-plus crowd is the fastest growing segment of the U.S. population.

Because of these factors, many financial planners say they won't even take on a client unless the person agrees to let the planner put together an investment strategy that goes out until the person reaches age 90 or even age 100.

In the past, people retired at age 65 and then lived maybe another seven to 17 years. But given modern demographic trends, the wise planner doesn't want his or her clients running out of money at age 82. (Besides, can you imagine the *guilt* those phone calls would trigger? Client: "You *promised* me I wouldn't run out of money, and here I am penniless, healthy as a horse, and *only* 89 years old!" Advisor: "Oh my goodness … I'm so sorry! I didn't think you'd live *so long!*")

The wise planner wants his or her client to be gone long before the money runs out.

Interestingly, though, when financial planners talk to their clients about planning well into the future, many investors respond with all sorts of reasons about why they don't need to plan *too* far ahead.

Kathy Boyle, a veteran CERTIFIED FINANCIAL PLANNER™ practitioner in New York, and the head of Chapin Hill Advisors, has heard it all. She's had clients tell her everything from: "Oh, nobody in my family lives to age 100!" to "Cancer runs in my family."

It's as if forward-thinking advisors like Boyle are betting that their clients will live long and prosperous lives, yet some investors are betting that they'll die!

Take the smart odds: bet that you'll live to be very, very old and gray. And do yourself a favor by creating an investing strategy that assumes you'll be around for decades to come.

$UMMARY $UCCESS $TRATEGY
TO CONQUER INVESTING MISTAKE #3:

Create a prudent asset allocation strategy. Studies reveal that asset allocation determines 90% of portfolio performance. Assess what mix of stocks, bonds, cash or other investments such as real estate are most appropriate for you in light of your goals, time horizon, and risk tolerance.

NOT INVESTING ON A CONSISTENT BASIS

Throughout this book, you'll read many accounts of investing moves gone awry. You'll also find a few stories that have nothing to do with investing per se. They do, however, offer practical guidance about how to conquer investing mistakes.

The first such story is a personal tale. It's about me.

IS THAT HOW I REALLY LOOK?!?

In early 2002, when I was a *Wall Street Journal* reporter for CNBC, I remember getting off the set after a long day's work, going into an editing booth, looking at a tape of myself and thinking: "I don't like the way I look. I look fat."

Sure, I'd heard that television adds 10 pounds to you. Still, I thought, I don't want to look *that* big on air! Seeing myself that way – through the unforgiving gaze of a television camera – was a big time eye-opener. At that point, I immediately resolved to lose weight – something that I'd never even given a thought to before.

For most of my life, I've known women who have battled obesity. I've also known waif-like women who dieted religiously and exercised like crazy. But I didn't fit in either camp. I wasn't fat and I wasn't skinny.

As a child, even though I was a bookworm, I'd been super active. I took ballet, tap and swimming lessons during grade school; I participated in sports and gym classes in junior high; and I was on the varsity track team in high school. As a college undergraduate at the University of California, Irvine, I played tennis only recreationally, but often enough to stay fit.

By the time I finished graduate school at the University of Southern California, however, my regular exercise was pretty much limited to walking up and down the steps to my Los Angeles apartment when I left and returned home each day.

WELCOME TO THE REAL WORLD OF DEADLINES

After graduate school, I entered "the real world," and started working as a journalist. After doing a stint as a reporter for the fast-paced Associated Press in L.A. – our motto there was "a deadline a minute" — I moved with my husband to Philadelphia. Though I maintained an impossibly hectic schedule – working at the *Philadelphia Inquirer* by day and at FOX-TV by night – large chunks of my days were spent sitting at a desk: on the telephone, doing interviews and writing news stories on a computer.

To make a long story short, my sedentary patterns started catching up with me. And my weight started mushrooming. I later had my first child, my daughter, just before I turned 30. And two-and-a-half years later, I gave birth to my son.

I reveal all this to explain that by the time I sat in that CNBC editing booth viewing myself on tape, truth be told, I *was* overweight. I just hadn't been paying attention.

But I was wearing a size 14 or 16 (depending on the clothing designer). I had not exercised in years. I rarely drank water, let alone the eight daily glasses recommended by doctors. And I was practically living on candy bars and vending machine food – despite the fact that I'm a vegetarian.

So what happened?

Simply put, I made a decision. At age 33, I resolved to lose weight to look better on television. (Yes, I admit that vanity was the driving force for my decision! But my secondary motives were to have more energy to play with my kids, and to not feel so sluggish and drained all the time).

Here's what I did.

I went to see a nutritionist. I read about seven or eight books on diet and exercise. I constructed a written plan. Then, starting in mid-April 2002, I got busy. And I mean ridiculously busy.

I worked out every day. I lifted weights. I cross-trained. I ran relentlessly on a treadmill in my house. (Sometimes, my husband actually had to tell me to give it a rest and let my body recuperate, because I'd want to work out in the morning and at night!)

All the while, I kept copious notes and charts of my progress. I also watched every thing that went into my mouth. I cut back drastically on carbohydrates, and (most excruciatingly!), I swore off sweets. For four months straight I did not eat any "treats." Not a single chip or even one bite of cake.

Can you guess what happened?

It probably won't surprise you to learn that I did indeed lose weight … 28 pounds to be exact. (My goal was 30 pounds. Truthfully, though, I don't know if I ever hit that target because when my perfectly adorable daughter – who was then four years old – started asking if she could weigh herself, I put the scale away; and haven't been back on one since).

I got down to a size 8 and was thrilled.

A year later, by the time I did my last report on CNBC in March 2003, I'm proud to say, I was still a size 8.

Friends, colleagues and viewers all noticed the change. Many people asked: how did you do it? I told them the key was just *deciding* to lose the weight, and then being *consistent* in executing my weight-loss strategy.

But can you imagine what would've happened if I'd worked out only sporadically? Or just quit exercising altogether after the first month? I can guarantee you that I wouldn't have had such drastic results in such a short period of time.

You know without a doubt that it would be foolish for someone to exercise once or twice a year in hopes of losing 20 or 30 pounds. Consistent, regular exercise is what would be required, among other things.

The same principle holds true for getting optimal investing results. Just like I couldn't get the body of my dreams without regular workouts, you can't realistically expect the portfolio of your dreams if you're investing only sporadically.

Nevertheless, scores of investors don't invest on a regular basis. They make the mistake of investing only when they have "extra" money. Some people falsely believe they need to have big sums of cash to invest, so they never get around to investing at all. Other individuals invest only sizeable figures on a yearly basis – using annual bonuses received from their employer or tax refunds they get from Uncle Sam. (By the way, I'm not suggesting that you shouldn't invest that IRS refund check or your year-end bonus. I'm merely pointing out that to invest with better results, it shouldn't be a once-a-year event. While we're on the subject, though, if you do get a big cash windfall, research shows that you're probably better off committing that money to the markets bit by bit, instead of in one lump sum).

There's another way that people exercise poor judgment in investing. Some investors flock to stocks or bonds only when they hear or read that the market is (or already has) moved upward. They want "confirmation" that the market or the overall economy is "strong" before they're willing to risk their money. Do any of these scenarios describe you – or anyone you know?

The problem with this approach is that when people fail to invest on a regular basis, they develop a haphazard approach to investing. They are inconsistent in their buying patterns and use a hodgepodge of criteria to determine "the best time to buy." They also become complacent about using proper investment strategies and they lack discipline. And finally, individuals who invest on a sporadic basis don't get the full benefits of compounded interest working in their favor.

I can't emphasize enough the financial harm that you do yourself long term by waiting to invest and not taking advantage of the power of compounded interest. To illustrate this point, assume you are 25 years old and plan to retire at age 65. If you socked away $3,000 a year for 10 years and earned 8% on your money, by the time you retired, you would have $510,090. Bottom line: your total investment of $30,000 gets multiplied 17 times. Pretty good, right?

Take a look though at what would happen if you waited 10 years to invest. In this scenario, you would start putting away $3,000 a year at age 35. And like most people who come late to the investing arena, you'd probably feel like you had to "catch up," correct? So let's assume that instead of investing $3,000 a year for just 10 years, as was the case in the first example, now you're going to invest $3,000 *every* year until you retire. The result is that you put away a total of $93,000 over the course of 31 years.

So how large does your pot of money grow? You wind up with $399,641 upon retirement. That's just over four times your total investment. Not terrible. But it's nowhere near as healthy a nest egg as you'd have if you simply started saving and investing earlier.

In the first instance, you end up with roughly $110,000 more at retirement. You also make annual contributions for only 10 years, as opposed to three decades. So you don't have to work as hard. On the contrary, your money is working hard for you.

When you invest regularly and consistently (now — as opposed to later!) it's like being in a 26-mile marathon, except you get to start at mile 10. That's

the power of compounded interest. It gives you a
huge head start so you can finish the race strong,
even though you're not working as hard at the end.

As the saying goes: "successful investing is about time invested
in the market, and not timing the market."

To remedy the error of investing on an inconsistent basis, or
to avoid it if you're new to investing, plan to invest every month
— or at the very least invest quarterly. Set up investment accounts
that are linked to your employer's payroll system or to your bank
accounts. Make investing automatic so that you don't fall into
the trap of halting your investment regimen amid periods of
heightened market volatility.

A systematic investment program also keeps you investing
during those months where you could use some extra cash and
might be tempted to forego putting money aside. (Admit it: If you
don't have an automatic savings/investment plan, it's awfully easy
to say something like: "Gee, I really need a new camera for our
vacation; I'll just buy one using the money I was going to invest.")

And take some comfort from people who have long had money
automatically withdrawn from their checking or savings accounts:
most of them say they no longer even miss the money.

In a rising market, another benefit to investing with regularity
is that you get to "dollar cost average." In dollar cost averaging, you
commit a specific amount of money at fixed intervals – regardless
of what the market is doing. In a bull market, dollar cost averaging
works to your benefit because it allows you to buy more shares
at a lower average price over time. This is accomplished because
you are "buying on the dips," or when prices fall, as well as when
prices rise.

In a bear market, though, where a persistent downturn is
occurring, some stock market experts liken dollar cost averaging
to throwing good money after bad.

And should you think about selling during such a downturn, be prepared for your financial advisors to try to talk you out of doing so.

In his book "Crash Profits," best-selling author Martin Weiss, who also heads Weiss Ratings Inc. in Palm Beach Gardens, Fla., suggests that stockbrokers will give you a slew of reasons as to why you shouldn't sell in a falling market. These brokers' advice ranges from "tough it out" and "hang in there" to "Don't be a fool and sell at the bottom," according to Weiss.

> All of this raises the question: should you invest regularly even in a down market? The answer is unequivocally yes. Here's why; later I'll tell you how. When you continue to invest through all market cycles you develop discipline. In fact, discipline gets imposed on your investing program even if your emotions start to creep to the surface.
>
> Also, you don't want to get in the bad habit of halting your investment activities every time the market hits a rough patch. If you do that, you're really just trying to time the market ... and how clear is your crystal ball?

Moreover, just because the broader market averages may be headed south, that doesn't mean your portfolio also has to go down. You can invest in ultra safe instruments, such as Treasury bills and other government securities. Weiss also recommends that you consider reverse index funds. They do the exact opposite of what the index they're benchmarking is doing. So if the S&P 500 Index falls 10%, an S&P 500-linked reverse index fund will rise by 10%.

You can also lighten-up on stocks and put more money in the cash markets. Better to remain a saver, and eke out even a modest return on your money, than to not put aside any money at all.

And in case you find this last bit of advice less than appealing, just remember that you're not alone if you are cautious about the equity markets, but continue to invest elsewhere. Even billionaire Warren Buffett, in his letter to shareholders released in 2003, said he was steering clear of stocks for a while because he saw limited upside potential. In discussing his recent performance, Buffett admitted that during "the last few years…my investment record was dismal." Buffett also said: "We love owning common stocks – if they can be purchased at attractive prices. In my 61 years of investing, 50 or so years have offered that kind of opportunity. There will be years like that again. Unless, however, we see a very high probability of at least 10% pre-tax returns (which translate to 6 ½-7% after corporate tax), we will sit on the sidelines. With short-term money returning less than 1% after-tax, sitting it out is no fun. But occasionally successful investing requires inactivity."

I doubt if many people would suggest that Buffett, who is clearly one of the world's greatest investors, is trying to "time the market." Rather, he's being savvy about where he puts capital – and in his case, it's very sizeable capital - at risk.

LABEL YOUR MOVING BOXES

To further increase your investing efficiency, earmark the funds you set aside as you invest regularly. So if you're saving an aggregate of $600 a month, that total shouldn't be thrown into one account and simply thought of as "investments."

Instead, you should clearly separate and label each account. If $100 is for your 10-year-old son's college education fund, have that money distinguished from your $300 a month retirement fund and your $200 a month account for the vacation you're planning two years from now.

Doesn't that make sense? After all, you label other things – from moving boxes to the seasonings in your kitchen spice rack.

Speaking of boxes, suppose you were about to move into a

nice big home. You'd spend a week or two packing up boxes with all kinds of stuff you've accumulated over the years – furniture, books, clothing, and so on. Now picture this scenario: the movers have come to haul away all those boxes, when suddenly you look down and realize that none of the moving boxes have been labeled. Yikes! You don't know which boxes are holding what. Is the china set in this box or that one? Where are your toothbrush, soap and other toiletries?

> Well, just as identifying your moving boxes allows you to readily visualize your household goods, "labeling" your financial accounts allows you to clearly "see" your investment goods. When you earmark funds – say, by specifying $250 a month for a new car in three years – you can also quickly and accurately measure your investment progress and determine whether or not you've met your designated goals.

There's another benefit to this strategy. If you or your movers came across a box labeled "spoons and forks," it would be obvious that the box should go into the kitchen, right? Similarly, labeling your investment accounts tells you where to put those funds.

And don't think it doesn't matter where you put your money, as long as it's invested somewhere. Nothing could be further from the truth. Financial planners say many investors who lump all their investments together frequently put the "right" securities into the "wrong" investment vehicle.

What do I mean by this? A perfect example of this is putting municipal bonds into Individual Retirement Accounts and 401(k) plans. IRAs and 401(k) plans are already tax-advantaged accounts. So if you place tax-exempt municipal bonds into those retirement accounts, you're not reaping the tax benefit of owning these tax-free bonds. In fact, you're converting tax-free income into taxable income because you'll later have to pay taxes on withdrawals from those retirement accounts.

Again, you might have the right investment – but be certain not to put it into the wrong account. It's kind of like having mislabeled the moving boxes, to take the previous analogy one step further. Wouldn't it be difficult (and frustrating) unpacking if you were in the kitchen surrounded by boxes that said "spoons and forks" and "pots and pans," but inside all the boxes there were really books for your home office and linens for the bathroom?

A PLAN BASED ON YOUR NEEDS

Raymond Lucia, a CFP® practitioner in San Diego California, has devised a unique method for having his clients "label" their money. His strategy is called "Buckets of Money™." Lucia, who wrote the book *Buckets of Money: How To Retire In Comfort And Safety,* suggests that you simply match your assets to your liabilities – creating "Buckets of Money™" to meet various needs.

"Buckets of Money doesn't involve some high-wire act like futures trading, currency arbitrage, penny stocks, or dealing in distressed real estate," Lucia writes. "You don't have to predict the future and you won't need to raise chinchillas, plant jojobas or be atop the crest of some so-called technological wave of the future. All you need to do is know your financial goals, divvy up your money accordingly, and then invest intelligently."

With the "Buckets of Money™" system, you purchase short-term assets, such as CDs and Treasury Bills and put them in "Bucket No. 1." That way you generate income for today.

Lucia recommends that you buy bonds and certain kinds of annuities to hold in "Bucket No. 2" if you desire inflation-indexed income "tomorrow."

Finally, he suggests that you acquire stocks and real estate in "Bucket No. 3" in order to achieve growth over the long-term.

Lucia reports that some 2,000 clients of his are now "bucketeers" – people who have "bucketized" their investments and reduced their portfolio risk as well.

$UMMARY $UCCESS $TRATEGY

TO CONQUER INVESTING MISTAKE #4:

Invest regularly with an automatic savings plan. Don't try to time market highs and lows. Commit to investing a fixed sum of money each and every month. Also, "label" your investment accounts to track your progress and know which funds should go where.

PART II

BUYING BLUNDERS

5

PURCHASING INVESTMENTS WITHOUT
HAVING PRE-SET BUYING CRITERIA

In the first section of this book, I walked you through some costly strategizing mistakes that ensnare investors. The next several chapters will discuss the buying goofs that all of us have made.

So let's start with a question: how do you currently decide which stocks, bonds or mutual funds are most appropriate for you?

Do you leave that to your spouse to decide?

Do you let your broker or financial advisor make the selections? Or maybe you actually research an industry extensively, and then pick what you think are the best companies in that sector?

Whatever investment-selection method you're using, I can guarantee you this: if you don't have established buying criteria, your investment strategy is off kilter.

Even if you've been successful at picking good investments in the past, invariably, at some point, not having specific buying criteria will come back to haunt you — for any number of reasons.

> Investors who fail to establish buying criteria inevitably end up purchasing the wrong investments. They are often unduly influenced by what others do or say. They're also more likely to duplicate their

investments, have an incorrect asset allocation mix, and suffer financial losses. Finally, investors who don't know why they should (or shouldn't) purchase a given investment have a much harder time later determining when to sell that investment.

Purchasing investments without some established buying criteria is akin to going shopping without a grocery list. If you didn't check the refrigerator and the pantry before you left the house, how do you know what you really need? Chances are you'll buy whatever looks good, or whatever you think is running low.

So there you are, pushing your cart down the aisle, and shopping without a grocery list. You see some item – maybe it's bread, eggs, or ketchup. Suddenly, you think: "Hmmm. Do we need more ketchup? Did we run out?" You go ahead and buy a bottle "just to be on the safe side." But then when you get home you find that you did, in fact, already have a container of ketchup – a full bottle no less.

The same type of foul up can happen with your investments. Without buying criteria, you can inadvertently duplicate your investments. You load up on things – such as small cap stocks – because you haven't checked your portfolio and you don't realize that you already own plenty of small-cap securities.

To avoid or fix this misstep, you must first know what you need – which begins with your asset allocation strategy. Remember the guidelines offered in Chapter 3 – with regards to selecting the right mix of stocks, bonds, cash and other securities? Once you have your overall investment roadmap set, you can drill down to the particulars: Namely you want to set criteria for buying stocks, bonds, mutual funds or other assets. In other words, what minimum set of hurdles must a company overcome to be considered worthy of your investing dollars? The idea is to establish some basic pre-requisites to weed out companies that don't fit your investing needs.

GENERAL STOCK-PICKING GUIDELINES

For starters, if you're evaluating individual stocks, start by analyzing the company's track record, history of generating revenues and profits, as well as its management expertise. For equities, also take into consideration a stock's price-to-earnings ratio and the health of the industry in which it operates. You should also be clear about the firm's competitive position. Is it the dominant force in the industry? Or is a small player going up against a number of much bigger rivals? All these factors, and more, will be important in helping you select investments that are in keeping with your overall asset allocation strategy.

And by the way, if some of these concepts are foreign to you, you're not alone. Nobody teaches you this stuff in school. In fact, Denis Walsh, of Money Concepts, says the lack of financial education in the U.S. is stunning. "It's shocking to me that you can get a degree, an advanced degree, and not know the first thing about how to manage money, let alone the difference between a small cap fund and a large cap fund."

To help investors, the National Association of Investors Corp. advocates the use of its Stock Selection Guide. The NAIC is an association of investment clubs. Its membership tops 600,000 investors who care – rightfully so – about investment education. NAIC members are encouraged to utilize research from Value Line in concert with the Stock Selection Guide. Even if you don't belong to an investment club, Value Line's independent research is highly valuable. (See more information on the topic of independent research in Chapter 25).

FIXED-INCOME INTELLIGENCE

If you are buying a company's bonds, or fixed-income securities, make sure you know the firm's credit rating as measured by Moody's, Standard & Poors, Fitch, or Weiss Ratings. What do these ratings agencies say about how reliable the company has been in paying interest to bondholders? Has it skipped any interest payments? Although bonds are generally less risky than common stocks, realize that bonds still have credit, interest rate and inflation risk. To educate yourself about various classes of fixed-income securities, visit the Bond Market Association at *www.bondmarkets.com.*

MUTUAL FUND BASICS

In evaluating which mutual funds to buy, you need to assess the fund's long-term track record. I would generally stay away from any fund that hasn't been around for at least five years; a 10-year history offers even better insights. You also should examine the fund's management. Who's running the fund you're considering? How long has that person been there and what's his or her philosophy? Additionally, how does the fund company go about selecting the companies in which it invests? Are securities selected by a single manager or does the fund use a "team" approach?

"I like seasoned managers," says stock-market expert Dan Strachman, the founder of Answers & Company. "Also, I don't care whether they pick Coke versus Pepsi. But I do care about the decision-making process they used to pick one or the other."

For mutual fund investments, you also need to think seriously about fees. Lipper Analytical Services is one company that tracks fund expense ratios. I'll discuss fees at length in Chapter 11. But for now, your primary consideration should be whether or not the fees the fund charges are reasonable or excessive. A good site for information is the Mutual Fund Education Alliance. Visit their web site at *www.mfea.com.*

QUANTITATIVE VS. QUALITATIVE RESEARCH

As you set your buying criteria, one decision you'll have to make is whether you want to rely on quantitative or qualitative analysis, or both. Quantitative, or technical analysis, refers to focusing on hard core numbers like sales, revenues, key barometers like price-to-earnings ratios, factors such as trend lines, and so forth.

For example, in 2003, the average S&P 500 stock traded at 32 times earnings – more than double the historical price/earnings multiple for stocks. If you are considering buying an S&P 500 stock and it's trading at only 14 times earnings, this data may give you insights into whether the company is reasonably valued.

Some say, though, that if you are a long-term investor you should rely not on quantitative measures, but on qualitative analysis. This simply means looking at the big picture. For instance, you might not know all the details about McDonald's market share, its average revenue per restaurant, and so on. But you may know, from a qualitative standpoint, that McDonald's is a fast food chain and that its brand name is recognized globally.

In this regard, qualitative analysis is more subjective. It's often easier to understand than quantitative inquiry. So if you aren't particularly technical, or if you don't have a lot of time, qualitative analysis may appeal to you.

$UMMARY $UCCESS $TRATEGY

TO CONQUER INVESTING MISTAKE #5:

Establish pre-set buying criteria before you purchase an investment. Pass on those investment ideas that don't fit your criteria. This will help limit unsuitable investments and guide you toward better-performing assets.

6

MISTAKE

RELYING ON TIPS AND "INSIDE" INFORMATION

Barbara Eng Nitzberg can still recall the first investment she ever made. It was back in 1989, and at her brother's urging she opened a Fidelity mutual fund account.

"I remember the check I wrote was the biggest I'd ever written," says Nitzberg, adding: "My hands were shaking."

By the mid-1990s, though "I'd become more knowledgeable and more comfortable with buying stock on my own," she says. But that also turned out to be the time she bought some of her biggest losers.

According to Nitzberg, who lives in New York, a big part of the problem was that she was getting – and acting on – bad advice. "I listened to people I knew, even if they didn't know what they were talking about."

Those friends and associates, however, were so gung-ho about various stocks that their enthusiasm was contagious.

"I tend to think it starts with a little dribble. Then all of a sudden everyone's talking about how wonderful this or that company is," Nitzberg says. "You get kind of caught up in that."

Nitzberg isn't alone.

Come on now. If we were forced to 'fess up, practically every investor would probably admit to having bought an investment – or at least having seriously contemplated doing so – just because a friend or someone we knew suggested it.

But this is almost always a bad idea.

> People who rely on "hot tips," pure instincts or so-called inside information often end up buying poor investments, and securities that don't meet their particular needs. Many times, these investments are also more speculative, volatile, and risky purchases. Thus, they more likely to cause investors to lose money.

It took Nitzberg awhile to realize that. But now she's glad she does her homework, and properly researches her investments.

"In the beginning, what I would consider looking at a company, was gathering company information. But I didn't know how to read a balance sheet. And I was too embarrassed to ask someone to teach me," she admits.

So instead she turned to companies' annual reports. But even there, she acknowledges, she didn't do a thorough job. "I'd read the nice part – the good glitzy part," of those fancy, colors reports. "Then I would go to two or three media sources and monitor" an investment before deciding whether to buy it.

These days, Nitzberg has a much better way of approaching investment opportunities. As a member of the New York chapter of the National Association of Investors Corp., she uses the NAIC Stock Selection Guide. "The Stock Selection Guide has given me a nice, standard, consistent way of evaluating whether something is a good prospect. Now I have a system," Nitzberg says. "It makes me feel more confident."

Among other things, the NAIC Stock Selection Guide lets you figure "the buy range" or the point at which you should consider purchasing a given stock. The Guide also aids you in determining whether a company is well managed. Finally, it helps you project sales growth and earnings per share for investments you are evaluating.

Nitzberg's story offers a valuable insight.

To put it bluntly: don't trust friends, relatives, colleagues, etc. to be your financial advisors. If they're not qualified experts, or if they haven't seriously investigated an investment, why should you seriously take their recommendations?

Taking a stock tip from a friend – even if it is a friend that you've known 20 years – is like trusting your barber when he says he can also install that new roof you need. What does he know about your roof – or any roof for that matter? You wouldn't want an inexperienced person fiddling around up there, because chances are you'd wind up with shoddy work. You'd want someone skilled and experienced to patch up that leaky roof.

The reality is that some things are best left to the experts. And I don't mean just financial services professionals. You too can be an expert – as long as you do your homework first.

Here's the best thing you can do when you get unsolicited advice from someone you think really doesn't know any more about an investment than you do. Nod your head politely, smile and let the information go in one ear and out the other. Now, if you think the person has good information, and presents you with some decent *facts* about why an investment might be a good opportunity, and you're interested, then take the time to do some research. There's no rule that says you have to buy today. Or that you have to run to the telephone phone and tell your stockbroker that you found a great new idea.

Take a breather. Evaluate the tip. And then see whether or not it's worth acting on.

And just like you shouldn't be so quick to follow a chum's recommendations, neither should you act on tips from strangers. And that's exactly what millions of people out in cyberspace are to you – strangers. Still, plenty of investors go into web site chat rooms and start to take advice from other participants. It's foolish because you have no way of knowing who is offering that advice. And even if they are qualified and credible, in how many cases will their mass-market prescriptions fit your individual needs?

THE RIGHT WAY TO USE THE 'NET

Having said all that, I'm not naïve enough to think that many of you won't turn to the Internet anyway. And, when done properly, that's actually a smart thing because the 'net is chock full of good information and educational tools for investors. In fact, Forrester Research predicts that by the year 2005, some 16 million U.S. households will get their first professional investment advice via automated online analysis. Another seven million households who use financial advisors will supplement that advice with advice from an online service, Forrester projects.

If you want to get online for information or advice, turn to a reputable site that specializes in this area. For instance, Financial Engines (*www.financialengines.com*) and mPower (*www.mPower.com*) are two well-known and trusted sources of retirement planning information.

Whatever you do, don't trust chat-room rumors, "inside" information from your broker or hearsay from your cousin Joe. Nothing other than smart, careful research should be enough to make you turn over your hard-earned money. You have to be willing to do the research yourself – or pay a professional to do it. When advisors suggest investments, make sure those recommendations are consistent with your overall strategy, risk tolerance and asset allocation plans.

When you research a company yourself, there are plenty of places where you can unearth information about a company's business prospects. A sampling of those resources: quarterly reports and other mandatory regulatory filings made with the SEC, annual reports and letters to shareholders, independent research and Wall Street research reports, and press releases from services such as PR Newswire and BusinessWire.

Another great resource to use is the Schwab Center for Investment Research. It consistently offers insights and information not found elsewhere. An example of these interesting tidbits: the Center found that for the two-month period from April until the end of May 2003, the S&P 500 gained nearly 14%. Schwab research suggested that similar returns were registered during a two-month period only 25 times since 1926, perhaps signaling a buying opportunity for investors.

Moreover, Charles Schwab & Co., Inc. gives some 3,000 publicly traded companies A, B, C, D, and F ratings. These grades give you an indication of what Schwab thinks of the companies based on four criteria: fundamentals, valuation, momentum, and risk.

Yet another online site worth examining is 3DstockCharts.com, which provides real-time charts of stock market buy and sell orders. The idea is to give investors a clear sense of what's happening in the market at any given time.

"Transparency and full disclosure are more important than ever," says John McNamara, CEO of 3DstockCharts.com

And again, while I don't suggest you spend your days glued to a computer screen, there is some valuable information to be gleaned here as well. For example, you can get real-time instant quotes. You can also see how many buy and sell orders are stacked up in a queue for a given stock. Perhaps chief among the highlights of

3DstockCharts.com's web site is that it has integrated data from all the major electronic communications networks, or ECNs: Island, Instinet, Archipelago, Redibook, Brut and the Bloomberg Tradebook. So you can instantly get from all the ECNs pre-market, regular, and after-market price changes.

INSIDER TRADING CRACKDOWN

What about getting tips from insiders who work at a company? Don't even think about it. First of all, if someone purports to know "inside" information about a company, what are the chances that you're the only person he's telling?

Besides, you don't really want engage in illegal insider trading anyway, do you? Federal securities regulators aren't taking such activities lightly, as evidenced by the prosecution of former ImClone Systems Inc. chairman and chief executive Samuel Waksal.

In June 2003, after being convicted of insider-trading, obstructing justice and dodging taxes, a U.S. District judge sentenced Waksal to seven years and three months in prison – the harshest penalty possible under federal guidelines. Waksal was also ordered to pay a $3 million fine, on top of an $800,000 settlement he'd made with the SEC to settle a civil lawsuit.

Not a fate worth risking, is it?

$UMMARY $UCCESS $TRATEGY

TO CONQUER INVESTING MISTAKE #6:

Thoroughly research an investment. Don't rely on other people's tips, idle recommendations, and so-called "inside" information.

CHASING THE LATEST HOT PERFORMERS

Going after the most recent investment "stars" causes investors to pay way too much money for what frequently turns out to be bad investments. In addition to risking market under-performance, investors who chase hot performers have difficulty selling if the investment turns sour because they're too concerned with "breaking even."

I can sum up this chapter in the following three paragraphs. But I'll go into more detail for those of you who really need convincing!

Here's the cliff notes version of this chapter: Don't flock to last year or last quarter's best-performing stock, bond, mutual fund or market index. Chances are, tons of other investors are too. Historically, investments on last year's "best performing" list wind up on this year's "worst performing" list. The Nasdaq Composite Index is a case in point. The technology-heavy Nasdaq rose roughly 86% in 1999. But in 2000, the index fell 39%.

Think about all the investors in Qualcomm Inc. who bought the stock near its peak. Many got caught up in the buying frenzy and investor excitement over this San Diego, Calif.-based maker of computer chips for mobile telephones. After watching Qualcomm zoom to $200 a share in early 2000, these investors spent small fortunes on the stock. Unfortunately, many also suffered losses of more than 50% when Qualcomm later came crashing back to earth.

Of course, Qualcomm wasn't the only such stock. Plenty of other companies watched their share prices travel the same upward trajectory – only to ultimately land at more realistic levels. In most cases, the stocks lost more than half their value.

But this is only really part of the story. Read on for more insights about the dangers of chasing returns – and how you can reverse this common investing faux pas.

DON'T GET TOO STARRY EYED

If you want to know about practically any one of the thousands of mutual funds out there, chances are Morningstar Inc. has detailed data on that fund – including its performance history, fees, the size of the fund, its investment objective and more.

But what Morningstar is best known for is its five-star rating system. In a nutshell, Morningstar assigns each fund it follows a rating of one to five stars. The rating is based on how well each fund performs compared to other mutual funds in the same category. Returns obviously matter, but so do fees and the level of risk associated with each fund, because Morningstar's rating system adjusts for both of those factors.

Having a top-rated fund from Morningstar gives a fund company or an investment firm major bragging rights. And when fund managers do climb into the top echelons of the Morningstar rankings, some companies spare no expense to let you know it. They take out full-page newspaper ads, they play up this information in quarterly mailings to shareholders, and they highlight their rankings in annual reports and prospectuses. Of course, they're very careful to

include the disclaimer that "past performance is no
predictor of future returns." Ironically, after all this
blatant hooplah — which demonstrates the extent to
which the Morningstar rankings are widely followed
and highly coveted –- most Wall Street experts will
turn around and tell you not to pay much attention
to such rankings.

I'm going to give you exactly the opposite advice, with several
caveats:
**Do pay attention to the Morningstar rankings, but don't be a
slave to them.**

You should never use one fact – a Morningstar rating or any
other single piece of information – as the entire basis for making
a decision as to whether or not you invest, or stop investing, in a
fund or stock. If investing is a puzzle (and indeed, it can sometimes
be quite mystifying), then consider the Morningstar ratings one
piece of the complex jigsaw you're working on. Also, don't invest in
anything unless it meets your established buying criteria and you
have properly researched the investment. So what if a fund has a
five-star rating? If you already have a similar type fund and are
achieving comparable returns, it's of little value to you.

**Realize how the rankings affect *other* investors – and
benefit from that.**

The truth of the matter is that even though investors are warned
over and over again not to chase performance, many people go
out and do it anyway. Invariably what happens is that top-rated
Morningstar funds will see big inflows of money because starry-
eyed investors were wowed by a fund's five-star status.

What many of these investors don't realize – or are forgetting or
betting against – is that historically, last year's star fund becomes

this year's laggard. So by jumping into a fund after it's achieved five-star notoriety, you're coming late to the party.

Dan Strachman, the Answers & Company founder, bristles when clients are eager to jump into a given fund just because they saw that it just won a five-star rating from Morningstar. "I say: What do you care what it did last year? You didn't invest in it."

Strachman, who also wrote the book *Essential Stock-Picking Strategies,* adds that "the problem with a five-star mutual fund is that all the data show that a four-star fund manager performs better" right after the rankings are released. The reason? According to Strachman, these four-star managers are hungrier and more performance-oriented because they now want to rise a notch and achieve five-star status.

Since Wall Street pros are vying to be in those top fund spots and touting that information when they do make it there, I think it's unrealistic (and disingenuous by some) to simply tell investors: don't pay attention to fund rankings. Which leads me to another observation about this subject.

Here's one big reason why the Morningstar rankings are so influential. In a world of more than 20,000 stocks and funds, investors want and need a way to cut through the clutter. Otherwise, many people might not have any clue about where to begin in the face of so many investment options. For their part, top-performing funds and fund managers also need a way to stand out from the pack. To attract and keep investment dollars, they must show how they are better or different from the next offering. So, in effect, the Morningstar ratings serve as a universally accepted short-hand; a quick and easy way to segment funds into tiers. And we can all generally agree on what a five-star rating means, just like we all know what an "A" grade symbolizes in school.

Both are simple, easy-to-understand ways to classify and categorize – explicitly singling out the star performers – at least by one given set of criteria.

FINALLY, LOOK AT RETURNS IN A DIFFERENT WAY

One way to put a fund's performance statistics in proper perspective is to view any given fund as part of your overall portfolio. Moreover, you'll want to start focusing on absolute returns, instead of relative returns. This means you want to generate positive overall returns in your portfolio regardless of the relative yields among different asset classes.

Adopting a strategy that focuses on absolute returns isn't very common. Most mutual fund managers, instead of trying to make you money year in and year out, simply try to beat a given index. So say that manager is benchmarking his performance against the Wilshire 5000 Index. If the Wilshire drops by 8% in a given year, but the portfolio manager steers the fund to only a 4% loss, you can be sure that the typical fund company, rather than decry the loss of funds, will position the 4% downturn as a victory in a tough market.

If you're going to start looking at absolute returns, you have to accept the fact that you will sometimes have down investments. Remember, if you've diversified properly you didn't pick investments that would all move in tandem. In fact, they should not be highly correlated at all. That way, when your bonds are faring poorly, you can probably count on your stocks doing well, and vice versa. With this method, you won't worry about the latest, best fund; nor will you participate in every stock fund or sector run-up. But you will achieve greater overall returns than you would've by trying to pick a single stock in a universe of thousands and "hit a home-run" with that one stock.

I'd venture to say that many investors in stocks such as PMC Sierra and Nvidia weren't thinking about absolute returns when they bought into these companies in 2003. These investors were likely chasing returns. By mid-year, both stocks were up more than 100% — a surge some saw as a sign of pure speculation.

I know it seems counter-intuitive, but many successful investors say that it's precisely the time that others are fearful of being in the markets that savvy investors will find buying opportunities. Conversely, when most investors are in a feeding frenzy, smart investors take that as their cue to sit on the sidelines and be very selective about their investments.

Here's some advice from one investor who learned the hard way about chasing returns.

IN THEIR OWN WORDS: INVESTORS SHARE LESSONS LEARNED

In younger years, I was a single gal earning a good six-figure income, working on Wall Street, living on top of the world, but clueless about investing. I devoured all of the investment advice that was available on the newsstands. I also didn't really understand why I was buying the stocks, bonds and mutual funds that my stockbroker was recommending, but obediently did what he instructed.

I thought that if I just bought the mutual fund that was at the head of the list that month, I couldn't lose. I would own this fund for several months or so when I realized it was nearer the bottom of the performers and another of the same mutual fund company's stock fund was now on top! Somehow, I always bought the wrong one at the wrong time.

What I know now is that I was buying a value fund *after* it had become a top performer and just before it was to become a bottom performer. Simultaneously, I was selling the growth fund to buy the value fund, as you now know, just before it went up! I was making one of the most common mistakes any novice makes.

The solution would have been to split my investment between the two funds and watch them slowly grow at different rates. Two steps forward, one back. Two steps forward, one back...

The biggest mistake was giving up on both funds, which are both still performing more than 10 years later. If I had known and kept both of them, this $10,000 would have been worth a lot more than the gold I invested it in! The funds would have been worth over $20,000 now and the gold is still worth less than $10,000.

I also know now that a good financial planner would have taken the time to explain all of this to me intelligently and I would have been better off for it. It's a mistake that I try to keep my own clients from making with their finances.

Mary-Jo P. Iacovino, AXA Financial Advisor
New York, NY

BEWARE OF PROMISES OF BLOCKBUSTER RETURNS

Sometimes, it's not just investors chasing returns of stocks and mutual funds that get them into trouble. Often times, investors seek out unrealistic returns elsewhere – only to get burned. Such was the case when a group of high net worth individuals handed over $900,000 to Eduardo McIntosh, a Boston area man later convicted of running an investment fraud scheme that cheated investors from all across the country.

In February 2003, McIntosh was sentenced to three years and one month in prison for taking investors' money, and promising them

40% returns on their money within one year, or five times their principal back within 10 days. Now what legitimate investment could "guarantee" such extraordinary returns? I certainly don't want to blame the victims here. But my point is that sometimes our desire to stretch for yield outweighs our common sense.

To test how much you know about investment scams, take the NASAA-CSA Investment Fraud Awareness Quiz at the end of this book.

$UMMARY $UCCESS $TRATEGY

TO CONQUER INVESTING MISTAKE #7:

Don't chase the latest hot performers. Last year's top funds are frequently this year's laggards. Better to look for investments with solid long-term track records.

OVER-EXTENDING YOURSELF
WITH MARGIN

Have you ever been in a retail store and wanted a new suit, a dining room set, or anything else you couldn't afford right then and there? For many of you, chances are that didn't stop you. You probably whipped out a credit card and paid with plastic, correct? In this case, what you really did was borrow money – maybe at 14% or so - in order to take immediate possession of whatever you wanted.

Well, in the investment world, the same thing is possible. You can borrow money in order to buy stock. It's called buying on margin.

Here's how it works.

Normally, when you buy stock you pay for that investment in full. But let's say you establish a margin account, and now you want to buy $10,000 worth of stock. Instead of having to come up with the entire $10,000, you could maybe raise $5,000 of your own cash, and borrow $5,000 from the firm where you created a margin account.

Investment banks and brokerages are willing to lend you the money to buy stock because they have collateral: the stock you purchase on margin, other assets in your margin account, and other funds you have on deposit with the firm.

Bingo! You're able to buy more and different investments without having to fork over as much cash. Sounds fine, so far, right?

The problem is that some investors unwisely "over-extend" themselves through the excessive use of "margin."

➡ Investors that are highly leveraged, due to too much margin, face a potentially crippling fate. If their investments or the overall market suffers a downturn, they could receive a "margin call" in which their broker sells securities in their portfolio or demands that they put additional cash into their accounts.

Unfortunately, many investors open margin accounts without fully understanding all the terms, ramifications and possible dangers involved.

Broadly speaking, here are some things you should know about margin accounts.

- **You can lose more funds than you deposit in the account.** If the value of the securities you purchase on margin fall below certain levels, your broker can ask you to provide additional funds to avoid the sale of your securities.

- **Your broker can sell securities without contacting you.** Don't believe, as some investors erroneously do, that your broker has to first telephone, mail or otherwise notify you about a margin call. The truth is that no such notification is required for a margin call to be valid. Now in practice, most firms will indeed try to contact you before they sell stock in your portfolio, but they don't have to. Besides, even if the broker does contact you, and you agree to meet a margin call by a certain date, the broker can still do whatever he deems fit to protect the firm's financial position, including selling your securities without notice to you.

- **You don't have the right to pick which securities in your account(s) should be sold in the event of a margin call.** Since those securities are collateral for the margin loan, your brokerage firm can legally decide which security to sell in order to safeguard its interests. This can be devastating if your broker sells some stock that you absolutely did not want sold, because of tax reasons or anything else.

Given these realities, here are some ways you can use margin wisely.

First, if possible, don't use margin at all. Again, think of the credit card analogy. If you're in a store and you have the cash, isn't it better to pay that way, than to incur interest and finance charges?

Second, know the rules that govern your margin account. In addition to certain requirements imposed by NASD Regulation, all brokerage houses have their own particular stipulations about their margin accounts.

Third, don't get over-leveraged. Do a "worst case scenario" calculation and determine a pre-set amount for maximum borrowing. Stick to this limit no matter how enticing the next investment opportunity appears.

In the best of all cases, you would never use margin if you didn't have the cash to buy stock. Does this seem contrary to the earlier advice I gave? Actually, it's not. What I mean here is that ideally, you'd only use margin if you have the money, but would prefer to deploy it elsewhere – to reap higher investment returns.

MARGIN MAYHEM THIS MILENNIUM

After the technology sell-off in 2000 and early 2001, investors nationwide suffered margin calls. Some who were especially hard hit had to sell stock from other accounts – thereby triggering unwanted taxes–in order to meet brokerage demands for payment.

Some of these investors were really just borrowing money to pay for stocks they couldn't afford – overvalued dot-coms priced at upwards of $100 a share.

And plenty of these investors found out another fact they didn't know about margin: that you are not entitled to an extension of time on a margin call. Sure, under certain circumstances, your broker may give you time to come up with the money to meet a margin call. But he's not obligated to do so.

To be as conservative as possible, remember to think about margin as kind of the equivalent of using your credit card to buy stocks. After all, credit is merely borrowed money. So you'd better use it wisely. And anyone who's dealt with credit card debt knows that it's all-too-easy to view that plastic almost as free money – at least until that shocker of a bill comes.

While some people might object, it's really not a stretch to compare margin to credit card usage. In fact, at some brokerage firms, if your account has a credit card or checks, you may also *create* a margin debit if your withdrawals (from checks, pre-authorized debits, or credit cards) exceed the sum of any available free credit balances plus your cash deposits on hand.

Another reason you should avoid excessive use of margin is that it may not just cost you money, it'll also cost you time. When you buy stocks on margin, you frequently have to spend a heck of a lot more time following your positions, monitoring your portfolio, and checking out the ups and downs of the stocks you own. Do you really want to spend your time that way?

$UMMARY $UCCESS $TRATEGY

TO CONQUER INVESTING MISTAKE #8:

Use margin wisely. Don't borrow money to buy stocks or other investments without carefully understanding the risks involved. And don't over-extend yourself by investing more money than you can realistically afford.

9
MISTAKE

HAVING CONCENTRATED WEALTH

Do you know what investments are in your retirement plan at work?

If you're like most people, you may own a big chunk of your company's stock in your 401(k) plan. You may not realize it, but you may also have created what's known in the financial services industry as "concentrated wealth."

Concentrated wealth refers to a scenario where an investor has far too much of his or her assets tied up in a single investment. The ill effects of having concentrated wealth are many: a lack of diversification, heightened portfolio risk, and market under-performance. Even after the high-profile blow-ups at Enron and WorldCom, where employee-investors lost billions of dollars, people still tie up too much of their money in one stock.

Workers at WorldCom saw the value of the company stock in their 401(k) plans dwindle to a mere $18 million in July 2002 from $1.1 billion in April 1999. Employees at Enron also lost a fortune. At Enron, 58% of plan assets were in company stock. That was like betting the house at the racetracks – far too risky for any prudent investor.

Of course, not everyone develops concentrated wealth simply by buying a truckload of stock in one company. If you have much of your net worth tied up in a single business, it could be that you inherited stock, you may have founded a business, or perhaps you amassed or were granted stock from your employer over time. However it happened, if you have a great deal of money invested in one company, you should remedy the situation immediately.

How much is "too much" invested in any one security? Most financial planners say putting 10% or more of your assets in a single company is courting danger. Others use a 25% threshold.

This single-stock phenomenon is apparently quite common. The Employee Benefits Research Institute says that company stock represents anywhere from 22% to 33% of the average holdings for people with 401(k) plans. Those numbers jibe with what other researchers have found. The Institute of Management and Administration's latest study of stock plans found that 27.9% of 401(k) plan stocks are invested in employer stock. And according to Boston Research Group, about 30% of 401(k) assets are in employer stock, and about 50% of those interviewed said they considered that stock riskier than money market funds.

Thus, even though investors know that pouring so much money into a single stock is risky busy, they nevertheless have not changed their behavior. And the consequences of this behavior – whether based on habit, denial, optimism or whatever – could be severe. "One of the biggest problems I have is to try and get people to understand and mitigate risk," says Ivan Gefen, a senior vice president with vFinance in Boca Raton, FL.

Professor Lisa Meulbroke, of the Harvard Business School, found that holding an individual stock is four to five times riskier than owning the Standard & Poors 500 Index. Her research also suggested that in order to compensate investors for the increased risk, company stock would have to be purchased 40% to 50% below its market price. That's a far cry from the typical 10% to 15% discount that some big employers offer their workers who want to buy company stock.

Various researchers over the years have demonstrated how owning a big chunk of a single stock can cause you to under-perform the broader market. A few samples:

- A November 1995 article published in *Trusts & Estates* magazine estimated that in a down market, a well-diversified portfolio might fall 9% or so. But the average single stock was likely to tumble 18%; and a risky stock was apt to suffer a 30% decline.

- A study in the November 1999 *CPA Journal* concluded that a $1 million investment in the S&P 500 from January 1970 through the end of 1998 outperformed a similar investment in the average single S&P stock by a whopping $18 million.

HOW TO HANDLE A SINGLE STOCK POSITION

One strategy to deal with a single stock position – and it's probably the one that will make you wince – is to sell some of that stock and pay the requisite taxes. While at first blush this may seem like the least attractive option, many experts say this is the best course of action when properly executed.

At Salomon Smith Barney, for example, specialists there who counsel high net worth individuals often devise what they call a "liquidation strategy" for their clients.

For some clients, they plan to liquidate 15% annually. And if the company's earnings grow 15% a year, in theory, the value of the investor's holding should gradually be replaced even while the client is simultaneously reducing his or her exposure to that one stock.

When you sell stocks in this manner, advisors often recommend that you re-invest the proceeds in a basket of diversified securities. You should also make sure you carefully weigh the tax consequences. This is an area for which you really want some professional advice.

CHARITABLE REMAINDER TRUSTS

You can also establish a Charitable Remainder Trust to liquidate big equity positions, diversify your holdings, and generate income. Such a trust works like this: Say you have $1 million in General Electric stock. And assume your basis in the stock is zero. If you sell your shares, you'll be required to pay 20% capital gains tax and you'd have $800,000 left over to re-invest.

On the contrary, with a Charitable Remainder Trust, you get to invest the entire $1 million in a tax-free environment. The way you do this is by donating the $1 million in stock to the trust. The trust, in turn, sells the GE stock. And because the trust is a tax-exempt entity, it pays zero taxes on the proceeds. You also get a tax deduction the year you fund the trust.

EXCHANGE FUNDS

Exchange funds represent another possible solution to the problem of concentrated wealth, though these vehicles aren't as popular as they once were. With exchange funds, you contribute your stock to a partnership, called an exchange fund. Other people do the same thing. Picture each investor as an owner of your own mini-mutual fund that you all have created. Every investor owns a bit of each company's shares.

The exchange fund then borrows money against the stock contributed and goes out and invests the money into an even more broadly diversified portfolio.

There is, however, a major downside to exchange funds. You have to stay in them for seven years. If you bail out early, you get dinged with a stiff sales load (commission). Another drawback: the partnership's holdings must contain at least 20% in any non-marketable assets, such as commercial real estate. Despite these disadvantages, for some people exchange funds may make sense to explore.

HEDGING STRATEGIES

What other alternatives are available to you to deal with your single-stock holdings?

For big stock positions, many say the best course of action is to hedge your position, and guard against a decline in the value of your shares. A detailed discussion of different hedging strategies is beyond the scope of this book. However, here is a quick summary of one popular way you can reduce the risk of having a concentrated equity position.

If you have $1 million or more tied up in one stock, consider whether it's worth it to cash out – without selling – by using so-called equity collars. A collar involves buying a put and a call at the same time, so you limit your upside potential, but at the same time you also limit your potential losses. (A put is an option that gives you the right to sell stock at a given price; a call is an option that gives you the right to buy a security at a certain price. Call options rise in value when prices in the underlying market go up. Puts gain value as underlying market prices decline).

Using an equity collar lets you lock in some of your profits and take a little cash out to boot, if you need to borrow money. However, these hedging transactions are subject to complicated "tax straddle" rules. Also, since many companies ban collars, you'd need to check with your firm to see if they would allow it.

Still, you should seek to reduce the dangers of having too much of your assets or net worth tied up in one stock, a situation that may set you up for a one-two knockout punch. If your company hits hard times, you risk your investment going down the toilet – and possibly losing your job.

$UMMARY $UCCESS $TRATEGY

TO CONQUER INVESTING MISTAKE #9:

Put no more than 10% of your money into any one stock, bond, or fund. Avoid "concentrated" wealth, where too much of your money is tied to one investment.

10
MISTAKE

LACKING TRUE DIVERSIFICATION

So much has been written about the benefits of diversification, that I think investors have a tendency to take it for granted. Please don't skip this chapter, thinking "yeah, yeah, yeah: I know I have to be diversified. I've heard that before." Trust me, you'll learn something new.

You've also undoubtedly heard the advice: "Don't put all your eggs in one basket." But to successfully navigate the buying phase of the investing process, you need more guidance than that.

You need more than just a basic definition of diversification. You really need to have a solid understanding of what diversification means, how it works, and how you can apply the concept to your portfolio.

To put it another way: Sure, you already know not to put all your eggs in one basket. What you may not know, however, is exactly where you *should* put those eggs – and how to handle your basket so that nothing gets broken.

This chapter will give you some key information in that regard.

HIGH TECH OR BUST

Back in the late 1990s, diversification to some investors meant having 10 or 20 stocks – and they all had to be in technology or have a dot-com behind the company name.

Nick Hodges knew plenty of those investors. Hodges, a CFP® practitioner who also has a CPA practice in Fullerton, CA, remembers a schoolteacher client planning for retirement.

The client's sister was also a CPA, and in 1999 "her sister was screaming at me for not investing her more aggressively," Hodges says.

The client, however, decided to follow Hodges' advice, and still invests $500 a month for retirement in a well-diversified portfolio.

"She stayed with me," Hodges says, "and she has an appreciation that her accounts didn't tumble like the rest of the market did."

Not every client followed his advice though.

Hodges also recalls a client with an $800,000 portfolio at the height of the Internet bubble. "He was very bright. And I tried to convince him that it was risky, and that he needed to be diversified," says Hodges.

But the client wouldn't budge. Instead, he took his money elsewhere.

"I talked to him months later, and his portfolio was at $400,000. Then another six months later, it was down to $200,000," says Hodges.

Of all the ominous threats that investors face, a lack of diversification ranks high on the list. When people don't diversify their holdings, they duplicate investments unnecessarily, have riskier portfolios, experience greater volatility and are more apt to under perform the broader market – especially during periods of economic uncertainty.

Are you too looking to "strike it rich" and make a big splash in the investing world? Be careful, lest you belly-flop, as this investor did, and likewise squander hundreds of thousands of dollars.

Fortunately, there's a better way. And for many of you – especially those who are new to investing – you get to learn valuable lessons about diversification in the best way possible: painlessly and free of charge. How so? You learn from someone else's mistake.

> If the stock-market meltdown that began in early 2000, the Enron scandal that cost many employees practically their entire life savings, and a slew of other costly investing fiascos have taught us nothing else, it is this: real diversification is more than not being too heavily invested in one stock, bond or industry. It also involves expanding your investment portfolio across geographic boundaries, market capitalization ranges, asset classes, and investment styles, such as value versus growth.

Let's look at each of these features in a little more detail.

IT'S GOOD TO GO GLOBAL

If you want a well-diversified portfolio, you need to think globally. Too many people stick close to home when it comes to buying investments. But getting exposure to foreign markets can provide a big boost to your portfolio.

"As an investor, you want to have as many ponds to fish in as possible," says David Winters, chairman and chief investment officer at Short Hills, NJ-based Mutual Series Funds.

Of its six funds, the firm has two international offerings: Mutual Discovery, a global stock fund, and Mutual European, a sector fund. "What we're trying to do is make sure that we find opportunities no matter where they are," Winters says.

Experts say that to be properly diversified, anywhere from 10% to 20% of your portfolio should be in international investments.

And some feel that buying international stocks also gives you the chance to buy investments at bargain basement prices. "We're very picky about what we buy, and furthermore, we're very fussy about what we pay for it," says Amit Wadhwaney, portfolio manager of the Third Avenue International Value Fund in New York. He's constantly on the prowl for solid companies that are based overseas, where Wadhwaney believes you can get much better values.

"Why would you want to pay two to three times more buying a U.S. company," he asks, "when you can buy essentially the same thing or something better abroad?"

WHY SIZE MATTERS

Beyond geographic diversification, you also need to make sure you buy investments in different market capitalization ranges. Don't fall into the trap of only buying one type of security: such as small cap stocks. Make sure you mix it up with mid- and large cap offerings as well.

Having various asset classes almost goes without saying. But it's worth noting because some investors can get themselves in trouble by sticking to one or maybe two asset types. For example, ultra conservative investors may stick to only bonds or perhaps bonds and cash. With this type of strategy, you risk inflation (and taxes) eroding the dollar value of your holdings. Conversely, some super-aggressive investors err by continuing to invest 100% in equities. If you're 25 years old, don't have any kids and are putting away the money for a long-term goal, such as retirement, you can afford to ride out short-term fluctuations in the stock market. So an all-stock portfolio may be fine. But for most people, with less tolerance for risk, or shorter time horizons, you'll want to have a decent dose of bonds, cash, and/or real estate as well.

Finally, make sure you're not wed to one particular investment style. Often times, when growth-oriented investing strategies are in favor, value stock-picking strategies are out of favor; and vice versa. So to make sure you minimize your risk – and still capture some potential appreciation – cover your bases by picking investments that use both investment styles.

If you tackle all these areas, then your portfolio will be truly diversified. And again, a tremendous plus to having a truly diversified portfolio is that a balance of investments will help you weather economic downturns.

THE LINK BETWEEN ASSET ALLOCATION AND DIVERSIFICATION

Vern Hayden, a CERTIFIED FINANCIAL PLANNER™ practitioner in Westport, Conn. says people sometimes confuse asset allocation with diversification. But he explains it this way:

"Asset allocation is a discipline," he says, where you divide up your portfolio into stocks, bonds, cash, etc. Hayden says then you drill down a bit and figure out investment style. In other words, determine what percentage of large cap growth funds is prudent, and so on. Then you go about "matching great managers of great funds to those allocations," Hayden says. "The result of all of that is diversification. And it has a strategy ring to it."

$UMMARY $UCCESS $TRATEGY
TO CONQUER INVESTING MISTAKE #10:

Get truly diversified to reduce your investment risk. Proper diversification involves spreading your investments among various asset classes (stocks, bonds, etc.) throughout multiple industries (energy, healthcare, banking, etc.), over market capitalization ranges (small, mid-, and large-cap), across investment styles (growth and value), and geographically (domestic and foreign investments).

11

MISTAKE

IGNORING FEES AND COMMISSIONS

Investors who disregard fees and commissions pay for that omission in diminished portfolio performance. Others simply pay too much for services that should be free or much less than they are getting charged. Small charges here and there may not seem like a lot in the course of one year. But over time, the numbers add up. The longer investors pay high fees, the more of a drag those fees are on investment returns.

UNDERSTAND THE BASICS

Before you can address the dilemma of high fees, you need to understand a few key things. First, you may have heard of an "expense ratio," but perhaps you didn't really know what it meant. An expense ratio is the fund's expenses expressed as a percentage of its assets. As a result, the higher a fund's expense ratio is, the higher its fees are.

You also need some big picture sense of where fees have been heading. According to industry data, fees rose steadily for the five-year period from 1997 to 2002. In 2002, management fees for large cap growth funds averaged 0.72% while large-cap value funds averaged 0.64%.

Additionally, you need a working knowledge of how mutual fund fees are imposed. By way of summary, here's a quick explanation of fees, delineated by share classes:

- ✓ • With front-end loaded funds, or class A shares you pay an upfront sales fee that is deducted from your investment. The sales charge isn't included in the fund's expense ratio.
- ✓ • With back-end loads, or class B shares, you pay no upfront fee. But if you sell before six years, you get hit with a redemption fee. Most B shares convert to A shares after six to 10 years.
- ✓ • With level loads, or Class C shares, you don't pay a front or a back-end sales fee. Instead you pay a higher annual fee.
- ✓ • With no load funds, you pay no sales charge at all. (But don't confuse that and think that there are no fees associated with your ownership of a no-load mutual fund). There are, indeed, other fees.

MONEY MARKETS ESPECIALLY VULNERABLE

If you're investing in money market funds with high annual operating expenses, you should really watch out. The reason? You might think you're getting a paltry 1% or so return on your money, but in reality, you could be yielding returns that are close to zero. Here's how: As of this writing – July 2003 – the Federal Reserve has the federal funds rate at 1.00%. (The fed funds rate is simply the interest rate that banks charge one another for overnight loans). And by raising or lowering the fed funds rate, the Fed is able to influence the money market arena – precisely the area that many individual investors (especially retirees) have money invested in taxable money market funds. Whenever the fed funds rate drops, so do yields on commercial paper, Treasury bills, and other short-term instruments.

Back in the late 1990s, the fed funds rate was a robust 5.5%. In 2000, it reached 6.5% - only to be slashed to 1.00% in 2003 as the Fed battled the economic recession. Nowadays, money market funds with yields of 1.2%, and a 1% expense ratio, are yielding a measly 0.2%. And if you take into account the fact that inflation is running at 3% annually, what you're really left with are negative returns, on an inflation-adjusted basis.

This issue is affecting millions of investors, given the massive amounts of cash sitting in money market accounts. As of June 2003, there was $2.1 trillion in money market assets, according to the Money Fund Report newsletter published by iMoneyNet Inc.

CRITICS ASSAIL HIGH FEES

In 2003, John Bogle, founder and retired chairman of the Vanguard mutual fund company, testified about this serious issue before Congress. "While the importance of cost applies to all types of mutual funds, it is most obvious in money market funds," he told the Capital Markets Subcommittee of the House Financial Services Committee. "Money fund performance comes down almost entirely to relative costs," he said.

In his testimony, Bogle related how 94% of the 263 taxable money funds for which he had data had gross annual returns for the years 1998 through 2002 of 4.6% to 4.9%.

Nevertheless, these same funds varied drastically in their fees, with annual expense ratios starting as low as 0.19% and climbing as high as 1.96%. Thus, the average net returns were drastically different: ranging from 2.6% to 4.58%.

Another telling statistic from Bogle: In 1978, mutual funds held $56 billion of assets and carried an average expense ratio of 0.91%. Today, the mutual fund industry boasts more than $6 trillion in assets, and the typical fund carries a 1.36% expense ratio. With a much larger asset base, one would think that fund companies could spread their fees over a wider pool of investors, thereby lowering mutual fund fees. Unfortunately, that hasn't been the case.

FEES UNDER SCRUTINY

But even before Bogle testified before federal lawmakers, mutual fund fees had drawn particular scrutiny. And the securities industry, under pressure to ensure fairness to investors, had begun to act.

In February 2002, the NASD announced the formation of a 22-person task force to recommend ways the mutual fund and brokerage industries could assure that investors are not overcharged when they buy mutual funds with front-end loads.

Usually, mutual fund companies reduce the sales load you pay as the dollar value of the shares that you or your family members own reaches specific levels, called "breakpoints."

For instance, take a look at the following breakpoint schedule, an example given by the NASD as guidance to investors:

Sample Breakpoint Schedule
Class A Shares (Front-End Sales Load)

Investment Amount	Sales Load
Less than $25,000	5%
$25,000 but less than $50,000	4.25%
$50,000 but less than $100,000	3.75%
$100,000 but less than $250,000	3.25%
$250,000 but less than $500,000	2.75%
$500,000 but less than $1,000,000	2.0%
$1 million or more	0.0%

Unfortunately, routine examinations by NASD revealed that investors weren't always getting the discounts due them. As a result, the SEC asked the NASD, along with the Securities Industry Association (SIA) and the Investment Company Institute (ICI), to take the lead in forming the task force. (The SIA is Wall Street's trade group, and the ICI represents the mutual fund industry).

Upon announcing the creation of the task force, NASD chairman and CEO Robert Glauber said the industry was "committed to helping investors receive restitution for missed breakpoints and ensuring going forward that they receive the discounts they are entitled to." He also said that "solving this problem is critical to investor protection."

To be sure, the issue of investors getting the discounts to which they are entitled is no small matter. As you can see from the chart above, if you were entitled to a 3.75% commission and you got charged 5% that was a sizeable hit.

Each mutual fund and family of funds set their own breakpoints and the conditions through which discounts are available. These terms and conditions differ from one fund to another, and they can also change. You can find out more information on breakpoints in the mutual fund prospectuses or Statements of Additional Information, and on many mutual fund company web sites.

To get a handle on this dilemma, the NASD required its member firms to do a self-assessment to determine how well these firms were complying with breakpoint reductions that should have been given to investors. As of this writing, the NASD was reviewing those self-assessments and determining how to best proceed.

WHAT CAN YOU DO?

Until the industry works this issue out, here's what I recommend.

- **Don't depend on your broker to give you the proper price breaks**. This is an area where you have to be proactive in seeking out and demanding the discounts you deserve.

- **Start by understanding how breakpoints work in general.** The NASD's web site, *www.NASD.com* is a good place for comprehensive information on this subject. Then look into how breakpoints are calculated and granted at your specific mutual fund(s).

- **Exercise your "rights of accumulation."**

  Did you know that you have something called "rights of accumulation" as an investor?

  A right of accumulation usually lets you receive discounted fees on a current mutual fund purchase based on a combination of that current transaction and previous fund transactions. The idea is that if your two (or more) transactions reach your fund's dollar breakpoint, you should be given a discount. For example, if you are investing $5,000 in a fund today, but previously had invested $20,000, those two amounts can be combined to reach a $25,000 breakpoint, which will entitle you to a lower sales load on your $5,000 purchase.

- **Write a Letter of Intent**

  It's very possible that you won't be able to immediately invest the minimum amount required to trigger a breakpoint discount. If that's the case, think about your investing plans for the next year or so. If you plan to make additional investments over the coming months (and remember the advice in Chapter 4 about investing on a consistent basis?), you might be able to get your fund company or investment firm to reduce your sales charges through a Letter of Intent (LOI).

  An LOI is a signed statement that you give your investment firm or fund company. This statement expresses your intent to invest an amount over the breakpoint within a given period of time specified by the fund. In effect, you're saying: "Look, I don't have a big lump sum to invest in order to get a price break, but I believe I should qualify for a breakpoint given the amount of money I will collectively invest" over the next year or so. Additionally, there's more good news concerning breakpoints. Often times, fund companies will let you include purchases you made within 90 days *before* the LOI is signed and within 13 months *after* the LOI is signed in order to help you qualify for a required breakpoint threshold.

A warning, though: If you fail to invest the amount stated in your Letter of Intent, and you don't hit the minimum dollar value for a breakpoint, the fund can retroactively collect higher fees from you.

- **Use Your Family Discounts**

The power and value of using your "rights of accumulation" or a Letter of Intent extends far beyond any one fund in which you might invest. These important tools can also be handily leveraged beyond what you, as one individual, can invest. When you exercise your rights of accumulation or initiate a Letter of Intent, you usually also get to count mutual fund transactions in other related accounts, in different mutual fund classes, or in different mutual funds that are part of the same fund family, toward your discounts. For example, your mutual fund company may give you a breakpoint discount by combining your fund purchases with those of your spouse or children. Also ask whether you can get credit for mutual fund transactions in retirement accounts, educational savings accounts, and even accounts at other fund companies or brokerage firms.

REGULATORS RESPOND TO THE FEES ISSUE

Because of "breakpoints" and other issues, it came as no surprise in June 2003, when the Securities and Exchange Commission released a 120-page report calling for better disclosure in the $6.4 trillion mutual fund industry. The same week, Rep. Richard Baker (R-La.), who is chairman of the House Financial Services Committee's Capital Markets subcommittee, introduced a bill that would require the SEC to adopt new rules on mutual fund disclosure. A key provision of the legislation would force fund companies to give investors more information about fees and fund manager salaries. For instance, under the proposal, fund companies would need to give you an estimate of your share of operating expenses, in dollar terms. Rep. Baker's bill also calls for fund companies to show portfolio transaction costs in a manner that would let you compare one fund to another.

While the bill wouldn't mandate that fund companies reveal salaries for fund managers, it would make fund companies describe how compensation is determined.

Regardless of what happens with the Baker proposal, or any related measures that are put forth, one thing is clear, this is an issue you must stay on top of.

WHAT ELSE TO DO ABOUT HIGH FEES

For starters, assess how much your broker is charging you per trade and what the true cost is of your mutual funds. Look out for 12b-1, or marketing fees, imposed by mutual funds. Also analyze what up-front sales charges (commissions) are being assessed, as well as any back-end sales load. To find some of this information, check the fee table in your prospectus or in the most recent shareholder report.

Be prepared to switch funds if necessary. Unlike switches among stock, bond and hybrid funds, if you bail out of a money market fund that's not a taxable event. As the price per share of money funds is always a $1 per share, you generate no taxable capital gains.

Look for opportunities to cut brokerage and administrative costs you may be getting charged. Enroll in Dividend Reinvestment Programs. Ask for discounts when your assets reach certain minimums (most often $50,000 or $100,000). Remember that fees eat away at your portfolio's overall return.

Be aware of things like inactivity fees, which are imposed on less frequent investors. These charges typically range from $25 to $50 a year.

Ask for a breakdown of fees: you'll probably be surprised to see the slew of fees you're paying. Often times, there are account set-up fees, especially at online financial institutions. Of course, you'll be charged per transaction fees, or commissions to trade. Then there are other occasional fees, like the annual custodial fee you pay for your IRA.

CONSIDER INDEX FUNDS

Outside of the money market universe, index funds are typically the least expensive of all funds when it comes to fees, since no active management is required. International funds are usually the most expensive of all funds. They require more work and due diligence – in the form of research, travel, overseas phone calls, etc. – on the part of the investment firm or mutual fund company.

Occasionally, you'll hear about a mutual fund company that is waiving its fees in order to attract new customers or to entice existing clients to invest a certain minimum amount of money. Take advantage of these opportunities when you can.

But also recognize them for what they are: inducements to get you to invest money – kind of like credit card companies offering teaser rates. In this case, of course, you're not taking on debt. But by making the comparison to credit card offers, I mean that the reduced rates and fees only last for a certain period of time. After that, the normal fees will be charged. So be sure you know how long your "no fee" deal at a brokerage or mutual fund company will last. And find out in advance of investing what the new fees will be once the "no fee" offer expires. You don't want to accept what seems like a good deal in the short run, if that deal ultimately is going to cost you more money in the long run.

Also realize that the size of a fund, the asset class involved, the portfolio manager's trading habits, investor turnover, and the fund's geographic focus all impact a fund's annual expense ratio.

According to Morningstar, for the five-year period from 1998 to 2002, here are the breakdowns for the average growth stock funds:

> Large-Cap U.S. equity fund: Expense ratio = 1.18%
> Mid-Cap U.S. equity fund: Expense ratio = 1.27%
> Small-Cap U.S. equity fund: Expense ratio = 1.39%

Expenses are slightly less for value funds:

> Large-Cap U.S. equity fund: Expense ratio = 1.04%
> Mid-Cap U.S. equity fund: Expense ratio = 1.22%
> Small-Cap U.S. equity fund: Expense ratio = 1.20%

Now go grab your most recent prospectuses. Go ahead – do it right now so you can check your funds. How do the fees you're being charged stack up to the norm? If they're excessive, or if they're unclear, don't waste time and money: Set aside an hour or so to talk to your fund company or to employ some of the strategies I've suggested above.

FEES AND YOUR 401(K) PLAN

And what about fees in your 401(k) plan? According to data from the Barra RogersCasey/IOMA 2000 Annual Defined Contribution Survey, 64% of employers cover all the costs related to a 401(k) plans' administration and record keeping. That means about one-third of employers aren't doing so. And only 21% of employers with plans that have $1 billion or more in assets pay all administrative costs. Translation: the employees of these companies are also paying those administrative fees. Yet, 401(k) plans also don't typically reveal their fees on your quarterly or annual statements.

But here's where some research and sleuthing can add some perspective. A study by Hewitt Associates, the consulting firm that specializes in pension information, found that typical 401(k) administrative fees ranged from $75 to $150 a year per employee. Meanwhile, the 401(k) investment management fees ranged from having average expense ratios of 1.04% (for U.S. small-cap stock funds) to as little as 0.49% (for money market accounts), IOMA data show. Compare that to institutional investors, whose fund expense ratios can be as slim as 0.1% after three years, and you'll see why you need to take charge in demanding lower fees. Granted, institutional investors wield much greater clout because they have far more assets than you do. Nevertheless, as your 401(k) continues to grow, you should continue to request fee reductions.

By way of additional guidance, the 401(k) Association says that all your 401(k) fees combined should not be more than 1% of annual assets. You can ask your Human Resources department to disclose your 401(k) fees. But don't be surprised if H.R. simply hands you a bunch of legal documents. Another way to find out precisely what expenses are being paid for, and by whom, is to log onto the Labor Department's web site. There you can download a copy of an informative paper called "Study of 401(k) Plan Fees and Expenses."

$UMMARY $UCCESS $TRATEGY

TO CONQUER INVESTING MISTAKE #11:

Pay close attention to fees and commissions. Excessive fees and high commissions can eat away at your overall investment returns – especially in a down market.

12

BECOMING OVERCONFIDENT

I love to watch sports – and not just professional athletes in action. Sometimes, I get a kick out of watching teenagers on a basketball court.

Ever notice how when some 16-year-old kid strolls on the court with a new pair of Nike shoes, all of a sudden he thinks he's the greatest thing since Michael Jordan? He'll say something like: "Watch me slam, man! I'll dunk all *over* you!"

That kind of bravado reminds me of what happens to some investors. When a bull market gets in full swing, they start readying themselves for the slam-dunk. They're not satisfied to invest consistently and methodically, to diversify their holdings, and to let compounded interest and time work in their favor.

No, that would be too boring.

This investor is always thinking that if only he had the right trading tools, if only he had certain key information, or if only he could make his own stock picks, he could outsmart the market. He's kind of like the amateur golfer who thinks that with the perfect set of golf clubs, he could beat Tiger Woods. And what are the chances of that happening?

What makes investors feel so invincible?

Terrance Odean, a University of California professor who specializes in behavioral finance, has done some fascinating research in this area. His findings are very telling.

> Individuals who get overconfident about their investing prowess can have that surge of self-assurance backfire on them. Overconfidence leads to poor decision-making, excessive buying and selling, diminished portfolio performance, and sometimes, financial losses.

To combat this investing faux pas, don't make assumptions about an investment. And please, don't be a know-it-all. Nobody can know everything about every stock or industry. Get help when needed, which is anytime you're even the slightest bit unsure about something or you don't have the time or the desire to learn about a prospective investment.

Interestingly, studies show that male investors express far more "confidence" about the investing process than do women. But very often women, research shows, tend to fare better in the investing environment. This chapter and chapter 22 will examine the role that overconfidence plays in portfolio performance.

Odean's research shows that people sell their winning investments more than their losing ones by a factor of about 1.5 to 1. Overconfidence plays a role in that, as do limited attention spans. Another contributing factor to overconfidence is the proliferation of all the information available to investors these days relative to previous decades.

Now there are financial news television programs, daily and weekly business newspapers, financial magazines, business talk radio shows, tons of Internet web sites devoted to investing, and the like. Armed with massive amounts of information from these varied sources is certainly enough to send your confidence into overdrive! But don't let your financial alter-ego – let's call it "Captain Crush-The-Market" — overtake all your good sense.

Yes, you may really be incredibly informed and knowledgeable. But it's foolhardy when you get so over-confident that if an investment doesn't pan out, you insist on being right – and declaring that the rest of the market is wrong. Your thinking is that somehow, some way, everybody else will come around to your frame of mind and your way of thinking. Well, if there were a herd of raging bulls heading in your direction, which would be easier to turn around: you or that entire stampede? It's so easy to get trampled by the market if you make the mistake of being over-confident. Try your best to be reasonable in your expectations and to keep your feelings of invincibility in check.

$UMMARY $UCCESS $TRATEGY
FOR CONQUERING INVESTING MISTAKE #12:

Guard against becoming over-confident. If an investment doesn't pan out, don't fool yourself into thinking that you're right and the rest of the market is wrong. The market is always right.

PART III

HOLDING/MONITORING MISHAPS

13

MONITORING YOUR
PORTFOLIO HAPHAZARDLY

Are you a person who likes to hold quarterly or annual yard sales? Or once a year, do you make a point to have a big spring cleaning – to get rid of the old clothes and stuff you don't really need? If you do, that's the same type of approach you should take to your investments. If you monitor your portfolio regularly you'll be able to see what you need, as well as what you don't.

On the contrary, not evaluating your portfolio on a regular basis can lead you to stockpile a lot of things you may not need – kind of like people who keep buying a new pair of black wool pants each winter, because they haven't been looking in the back of their closet, where there are seven other pairs of black wool pants.

I'll admit, I'm certainly a person who grapples with this one: the mistake of not monitoring my portfolio regularly enough.

If you're in the same boat, it's time for a life jacket.

When investors fail to adequately monitor their portfolios, they lose track of what they own, they forget why they even hold certain investments, and they maintain investments that are no longer appropriate.

There's another danger to haphazardly monitoring your investments. Most brokerages and investment banks require you to dispute any transactions within 30 days of receiving an investment statement. So, if your broker (or someone else) initiates a transaction that you didn't authorize, how would you know about it if you don't review your statements?

Checking those statements carefully when you get them will allow you to unearth any possible errors.

That's what happened to Margaret Bongiorno. One day she got a statement in the mail indicating that her broker sold $2 million worth of Sarah Lee stock that was in Bongiorno's account. At the time Bongiorno was an 84-year-old housewife from Long Island, N.Y. She denied giving her broker permission to sell the stock and the two sides wound up in arbitration. Thanks to her daughter, who was reviewing her mother's mail, Bongiorno knew about the transaction. But if she hadn't checked her statement she wouldn't have discovered the sale. So clearly, reviewing investment statements is especially important to check for mistakes and to make sure brokers aren't doing anything contrary to your wishes.

Here's another account from an investor who was wronged by a broker – but didn't find out about it until it was too late.

IN THEIR OWN WORDS: INVESTORS SHARE LESSONS LEARNED

After much persistence from a financial advisor with (a Wall Street brokerage), I rolled over my IRA and opened a Money Market Account. Initially my account was handled with care and I had consistent contact with my advisor. My portfolio grew and I was happy. I trusted my advisor and the company she represented. Suddenly, she moved to New Jersey and was having personal problems. Unfortunately, I was not aware that she had made my portfolio very heavy in technology. Well, as we all know the market took a sudden turn and I lost many, many $$$$. (I had signed documentation to state I only wanted medium risk). I should not have been placed in a high-risk situation.

I made many attempts to contact my advisor and my calls were not returned. I contacted the company and advised them that I felt my account was being mishandled. I was bounced from office to office. At this time I also noticed that my Money Market account had dwindled. Why, I asked myself? I had never withdrawn a dime. Finally, I am contacted by my advisor, who now surfaced in California. I confront her with my anger and anguish over the tremendous loss in my portfolio and the absence of $21,000 in my Money Market account. I checked over statements that had arrived and found the word "MARGIN" connected with my account. I was totally perplexed, as I honestly didn't have a clue what this meant. After investigating and searching on the Internet I found that she had purchased tech stock on margin. I never signed any paperwork that authorized her or the company to do such transactions. The CA office assured me that these funds would be returned. Well, I waited and nothing happened. My account was returned to NY for handling and a high-ranking individual at the company advised me that I should acquire a lawyer immediately. I acquired a lawyer and after much back and forth was given a settlement. It was not to my liking but it was better than nothing.

The lawyer does not give me the proper information on how this settlement should be handled and I end up paying the lawyer a third, IRS a third and me a third. It was one nightmare after another. I lost approximately $175,000.00, three years of mental anguish and lack of sleep. I learned to NEVER trust anyone, especially the big corporations. I felt that the company should have been held more accountable for their lack of supervision on the handling of my accounts. The lawyer should have been held accountable for misinforming me and causing me further monetary loss and sleepless nights.

Unfortunately, during the time that this was all happening I had severe illnesses in the family, which ended in death, and I did not give my portfolio my undivided attention. I stupidly felt that the company and the lawyer had my best interests at heart! These were very bitter lessons that I learned: not to trust anyone but yourself! I was made a fool of two times, but rest assured it won't happen a third.

V.B., Ridgewood, NY

I know that in down markets in particular, the temptation is to file those statements away without even opening them. I once interviewed a woman in her 50s who was a long-time employee of a telephone company. In 2002, she stopped looking at her quarterly statements because every time she got one, it showed her retirement money had fallen by another $10,000 or $20,000. (She ultimately moved into annuities and says she feels less stressed about her investing).

But what she did – in terms of not looking at those statements — was actually very common.

So common, in fact, that Charles Schwab & Co., Inc. implemented a "Fresh Start" program in early 2003. The company found that scores of investors were simply stashing those statements in their drawers and not opening them. "Many people were just frightened and confused," company founder Charles Schwab told me during an interview. He said the goal of the program – where new clients could sign up for a free portfolio evaluation – was to get people to intelligently review their portfolio status, and to make changes if necessary. Simply ignoring a declining portfolio, he noted, would be a "big mistake."

So don't just stick your monthly or quarterly statements into a file (or worse yet, the trash) and never look at them.

- Open those statements.

- Check out your portfolio at least every six months, preferably quarterly to monitor performance and look at the underlying fundamentals of your investments.

- Also establish a system for regularly reviewing your investments. It could be a beginning of the year, mid-year or end of year assessment.

- Make a point to systematically check out everything in your portfolio.

- Ask yourself if the reason you bought an investment remains valid.

    None of this is to suggest that you should obsess over the quarterly fluctuations in your portfolio. After all, it's senseless to get bent out of shape based on a three-month time period in your 20 or 30 year investing plan. But if you stay on top of your investment portfolio with annual check-ups, you'll be more relaxed about your overall investing experience. And you'll find that there's no need to obsess over either the daily volatility in the stock market or quarterly blips.

$UMMARY $UCCESS $TRATEGY

TO CONQUER INVESTING MISTAKE #13:

Monitor your portfolio on a regular basis. Open your statements and review them. Check for errors. Make sure you've authorized any transactions that occurred. Don't just throw your monthly, quarterly or annual statements into a drawer or in the trash can.

HAVING YOUR ASSETS SPREAD OUT OVER TOO MANY ACCOUNTS

When scores of investors lost money in their 401(k) plans for the first time in 2001, some blamed employers who didn't offer enough variety in their retirement offerings to shield employees from the struggling economy. For example, out of every five 401(k) plans, only two had a small-stock fund option.

But sometimes, having too many accounts can also hurt your investing strategy.

> Having too many investment accounts makes it far too easy for investors to lose track of what they've bought, duplicate their investments, pay too much in fees, and thwart their asset allocation goals. All of this can lead to generating poor investment returns. A multitude of accounts creates extra headaches during tax season. There's an emotional downside to this mistake too: getting overwhelmed, and feeling stressed about a lack of control over your investment portfolio.

The Investment Company Institute says there are 95 million mutual fund shareholders in 54.2 million U.S. households. As of

May 2001, the latest for which figures were available, the average U.S. household had $119,700 in assets spread out among six mutual funds. What's appropriate or ideal?

Here are some ideas on this topic from money management pros. Be prepared, because their advice runs the gamut.

Rande Spiegelman, a CERTIFIED FINANCIAL PLANNER™ practitioner in San Francisco, says many investors are best served by owning just one index mutual fund, such as those that mimic the performance of the Wilshire 5000 Index. With this type of fund, Spiegelman reasons, you'll be getting broad stock-market exposure, including an array of small-, mid-, and large-cap companies.

By contrast, Alexandra Armstrong, a partner at the Washington, D.C. investment advisory firm Armstrong Welch & MacIntyre, says that 10 or 15 funds are entirely appropriate – for those with at least $1 million in assets.

These and other financial advisors say they've encountered some clients whose portfolios are completely out of control, with upwards of 30 or 40 funds. And sometimes the investors don't have the asset size to justify this extremely large number of accounts.

SOME SIMPLE SOLUTIONS

Having your investments spread out over too many accounts is, quite literally, spreading yourself to thin. Don't try to be a super-hero and manage an overwhelmingly complex set of holdings.

- If you think the number of funds you own have gotten unwieldy, consolidate if necessary.

- If appropriate, consider index funds or build your own core portfolio of diversified mutual funds and/or individual stocks, bonds and funds so that there's no need for 10 or 20 miscellaneous accounts.

- You can also look into Spyders, Diamonds and QQQs. Don't let the names throw you. These are just the index-tracking stocks for the S&P 500, the Nasdaq, and the Dow Jones Industrial Average, respectively. If you buy these investments, you'll be getting broad exposure to the market and again, you may not need to have a multitude of other funds.

A HIDDEN DANGER

Michael Kresh, of MD Kresh Financial Services, says he sees too many people who come into his office and "don't understand what they own." As a result, he warns that you shouldn't lose sight of a bigger problem caused by excessive funds: duplicating your investments. "The single biggest issue is portfolio overlap," Kresh says. "I'm more concerned about the amount of overlap than I am about how many funds you own."

$UMMARY $UCCESS $TRATEGY
TO CONQUER INVESTING MISTAKE #14:

Maintain a manageable number of mutual funds. There's no "right" number that's suitable for all investors. But if you spread your assets over too many accounts, you may pay excessive fees, get overwhelmed with statements, or duplicate your investments.

FAILING TO REASSESS AND REBALANCE
YOUR PORTFOLIO AS NEEDED

No one has to tell you to take your umbrella with you outdoors if you see threatening rain clouds. Not to do so just because you're in a rush to get out of the house would be short-sighted, right? By the same token, you have to check the weather, so to speak, with regard to your investment portfolio. When external forces shift, it's often prudent for you to reassess whether your portfolio also needs shifting.

Those investors who bypass such a review risk under-performing the market, taking on additional portfolio risk, hanging onto to inappropriate investments and possibly having improper asset allocation.

You should also be aware that sometimes one investment you own performs really well and begins to take up a larger percentage of your portfolio than intended. If this occurs, make sure you re-jigger that position so that the amount you own in any one stock or asset class is consistent with your intentions. You don't want even "good" investments to throw your asset allocation strategy out of whack.

According to Michael Kresh, of MD Kresh, "one of the reasons why investors have performed so much worse than expected is because a lot of funds allowed their stock positions to become very similar." With regards to the funds he picks, "We're very cautious about whether these fund managers really do have very different styles," Kresh notes, citing one fund that looks for broken down bonds and deep value, while another one seeks growth at a reasonable price.

> Ibbotson Investment Research has long shown the benefit of rebalancing. If nothing else will get you to rebalance your portfolio, perhaps this statistic will: During the past 25 years, rebalancing at least once a year on a portfolio with a target split of 60% stocks and 40% bonds cut the risk of the portfolio by nearly 20%.

Remember: You're starting with your investing plans as broadly laid out in your asset allocation strategy. When you get down to diversification, those plans are merely guidelines. They've got to have some wiggle room in them because circumstances invariably change.

TAKE A LOOK AT RISK

As you monitor your portfolio, one key factor you want to check is how much risk your investments possess. Surely you know about volatility, as triple-digit point swings on the Dow Jones Industrial Average seem to be commonplace now. But given the market's gyrations, you really need to get a handle on how risky your unique holdings are. One company that can help you determine this is RiskMetrics, a J.P. Morgan spin-off. The firm's web site, *www.riskgrades.com*, will "grade" the riskiness of any stock and most mutual funds.

FAVOR LOW BETA STOCKS

A stock's beta is simply a measure of its volatility, compared with a given benchmark. The most frequent benchmark investors use is the S&P 500 Index. If you have a stock with a beta of 1.0, that means it matches the volatility of the broader index. Any stock with a beta that is greater than 1.0 will experience more gyrations than the overall market, in both good and bad times. A stock with a beta of less than 1.0 will be less volatile than the general market.

So let's say you own a low-beta stock. It's a company with a beta of .75. When the market goes up or down, the stock will move in the same direction, but only 75% as much. Therefore, if the S&P 500 climbs 10% this same stock would go up by 7.5%. By the same token a 10% drop in the S&P 500 would produce only a 7.5% fall for this stock. What you need to take away from all this is that you should seek out low beta stocks if you want to minimize your worries about risk as you monitor your portfolio. You can visit S&P's Personal Wealth web site (*www.personalwealth.com*) (it's run in conjunction with BusinessWeek magazine), or Multex Investor (*www.multexinvestor.com*) to check the beta of any stock. Multex is a Reuters service that provides financial research and information.

Hugh Johnson, market strategist at First Albany, once told me that one smart way people can rebalance their investments wisely is to diminish risk in their portfolios. He suggested buying sectors of the market that are typically less volatile, such as health care, utility, and consumer-staples industries.

CHANGE WITH A PURPOSE

Don't make changes to your portfolio just for the sake of changing. And I'm certainly not advocating wholesale liquidating of your investments. However, you should certainly revisit your plan on a regular basis. Re-evaluate things. Think about it this way: If you buy a new car, it's great in the beginning. But after a while, the tires get a little worn. You have to change the oil, maybe put on a new pair of brakes. Your investment portfolio works the same way.

Companies change, markets change, and so do industries. What worked for you five years ago may not be as compelling today.

Make a point to re-examine your investments whenever broad economic conditions transform, industry conditions are altered, or major changes occur at the company in which you're investing. Some things to think about: Has the manager of that mutual fund you bought seven years ago left? Has a company's credit ratings been downgraded or have its financials began to deteriorate? Is the industry, in general, under pressure? These are some of the considerations worthy of your attention when you start to consider if it's time to rebalance your portfolio.

$UMMARY $UCCESS $TRATEGY

TO CONQUER INVESTING MISTAKE #15:

Rebalance your portfolio as needed. Your asset allocation can get out of whack if certain investments start to represent a larger portion of your overall portfolio than you intended.

16

FAILING TO ACT WHEN YOUR PERSONAL SITUATION HAS CHANGED

The previous chapter talked about how and why you might need to tweak your investment portfolio if external factors change. This chapter is designed to get you thinking about smart ways you should be monitoring your portfolio if your personal situation changes.

If you remind yourself to consider your finances whenever you have a major event in your life – either personally or professionally – chances are you'll do a decent job of holding the proper investments.

> You should reassess your investments if you have a major personal or professional event. For instance: have you gotten married, had a child, or planned a new business venture? These are some reasons to reconsider your investment holdings and make sure they're right for the current time.

Investors who fail to re-evaluate their investment holdings when important changes have occurred in their lives may hold securities that are no longer appropriate for their needs. These investors also suffer from improper asset allocation.

If your review suggests that it's time to lighten up on a given investment, make preparations to do that. Discuss tax implications with your tax advisor. Consider what better-performing investment alternatives are available to you, and so forth. When you are successfully holding and monitoring your investments, you want to cull from your portfolio, not engage in wholesale selling.

Don't overdo it on either side – in terms of buying investments and keeping them forever, or selling them when you really should hang onto them.

Though some big-name investors have made a fortune by buying and holding, chances are you'll have to liquidate your holdings at some time. Warren Buffett is famous for saying he likes to "buy and hold forever." With his wealth, he certainly has that luxury. Most people don't.

Whatever you do, avoid the mistake that some investors make when they monitor their portfolios obsessively: these investors wind up going way overboard in switching in and out of stocks for all manner of reasons.

HOLDING PERIODS ON THE DECLINE

Just look at what happened during the Internet bubble.

According to research from Boston-based consulting firm Bain & Co., shareholders of many Internet companies typically hung onto their stocks for just a few days at a time. And that includes those Internet companies that are still around today like Yahoo!

Even larger, blue-chip companies had less loyal investors. Back in 1999, the average IBM shareholder owned Big Blue for just 9.2 months. Johnson and Johnson shareholders owned that company for 23.4 months before selling. And General Electric shareholders had an average holding period of 30.2 months.

The following data illustrate how investors are hanging onto stocks for less and less time.

Holding Period For Average Stock on NYSE

Year	Holding Period
1960	8.3 years
1970	5.3 years
1980	2.8 years
1990	2.2 years
2000	1.3 years

Source: Bain & Co.

To stay on top of when you might need to more actively monitor your portfolio, you might create a "life events" checklist or get one from a financial planner. This life events checklist is designed to get you to think about changes in your life that you have already experienced, or may experience in the future – changes that can have relevant financial and investment planning implications.

$UMMARY $UCCESS $TRATEGY
TO CONQUER INVESTING MISTAKE #16:

Change your investments when your personal situation or goals change substantially. If you experience a major life event, such as having a baby, getting married, or starting a business, assess whether your investments need updating.

PART IV

SELLING SNAFUS

17
MISTAKE

NOT HAVING A SELL STRATEGY

There comes a time when every investor, from the novice to the sophisticated professional, must confront this question: Should I sell or should I hold?

For a lot of investors, this is one of the most agonizing decisions they make. It's so agonizing, in fact, that some don't make a decision at all – or they do so only by default. They *know* they should sell, or they *think* they should, but somehow they can't bring themselves to do so.

Indeed, the whole area of selling seems to be the greatest source of anxiety for investors. There's good news and bad news on this front. The bad news is that selling mistakes can cost you a fortune.

The good news is that you can conquer this problem. Over the course of the next few chapters, I'll tell you how. Before I do, though, a few observations.

Investors who lack a sell strategy are baffled about what investments to sell and why. Fear and other emotions guide their decisions. They often follow the herd and make poor decisions, such as dumping a stock prematurely or selling amid a market panic.

After considering your personal needs, investment philosophy and leanings, come up with a set of rules to guide why, when and under what circumstances you will sell a stock.

This creation of a selling strategy must be done at the outset – prior to buying a stock!

If more investors followed this simple rule, they would have a lot easier time down the road in determining when to hang on to investments and when to let them go.

For those stocks, bonds, currencies or other investments you already own, establish a sell strategy now to guide decision-making going forward.

And plan to give your selling strategy the proper time and attention it deserves.

> A study by Roper/Ameritrade survey found that consumers spend an average of 7.6 hours researching each investment they purchase. But precious little time and thought are given to the sell decision.

Some experts believe that almost any carefully thought out strategy can be workable. The key is to have some pre-established idea of what you will do, when you would do it, and why, under various circumstances. Of course, no one has a crystal ball. So your sell strategy isn't supposed to cover every possible scenario. But by and large, you should be able to assert what you would do given, say, a big run-up in your investments or big losses as well. When financial markets experience extreme volatility, as has been the case for the past decade, having a selling strategy becomes even more important. Otherwise, the topsy-turvy nature of the market may cause you to act impetuously.

Intellectually, most investors know that selling amid a market panic is a bad idea. Nevertheless, many people fall victim to this blunder. Often times, when broad based selling is occurring, it's because the individuals involved didn't have a plan. As a result, they are just following the herd.

But if you take a look at past stock-market trends, it's plain to see that dumping stock in a market sell-off typically has been a wrong move. The reason is because most investors don't know when to jump back into the markets. And those investors who pulled out of the financial markets after big market declines lost out in a big way.

> For example, if you stayed invested in the S&P 500 Index for the entire 2,528 trading days from 1980 through 1989, you would've racked up 17.5% average annual returns. But if you pulled out of just 10 of the best trading days during that decade, your average annual return got chopped down to 12.6%. People who missed the best 40 days during that 10-year span had a return of just 3.9%, according to Ibbotson Associates.

This is not to suggest that no matter what, you should always stay fully invested in equities – even when you are not comfortable doing so. On the contrary, your selling strategy should also fit nicely with your overall investing game plan. In other words, you should be able to sleep at night with whatever sell strategy you devise, as it pertains to your risk tolerance, time invested in the market, and so on.

Some smart selling strategies include employing 30-day moving averages, using stop-loss mechanisms, and relying on fundamental research, among others. When you use a stock's 30-day moving average as a guidepost for selling, you sell when it consistently falls below its trend, that 30-day average. Some investors also use 60 and 90-day moving averages to guide them.

A stop-loss mechanism helps to make selling automatic. And that's a big plus for many investors. A stop order puts a "floor" or a "ceiling" that defines when you will sell a security. So, if you buy a stock at $25 a share, you might put a floor at $17.50. What this means is that you're not willing to lose any more than 30% of your money. So if that $25 stock fell by $7.50 (or 30%) to $17.50, a sell order would automatically be triggered. On the upside, you could also put in a 30% ceiling. In this case, if the stock hits $32.50 a sell order would also be instantly triggered, letting you lock in your profits. Other people have less technical, though equally effective methods for investing successfully at the selling phase.

An example comes from trader Susan Kingsbury, who lives near Salt Lake City, Utah. In discussing her selling strategy, she once told me that she's able to sell her losing investments because she views them simply as "a cost of doing business." In that way, Kingsbury suggested she's able to take her lumps when need be without feeling so emotionally wracked over her decision to sell.

Here are three web sites that can help you calculate when it's time to sell a stock:

www.dynamictaxoptimizer.com

www.quicken.com

www.networthstrategies.com

Dynamic Tax Optimizer is a finance and accounting calcula- tor engine that aids you in making selling decisions by showing you which decisions will result in the optimal after-tax returns. David Gottstein, head of Anchorage, Alaska-based Dynamic Capi- tal Management, believes the tax-loss harvesting feature his firm offers makes it of particular value to investors who are deciding what to sell and when.

Another company, Smart Leaf (*www.smartleaf.com*) makes soft- ware that it sells to financial services professionals. That software helps your advisor recommend when a stock should be sold and when it should be kept. Smart Leaf CEO and founder Jerry Michael once explained to me that in making any educated sell decision, you really have to balance risk, taxes, your own estimate of future returns, as well as expenses.

$UMMARY $UCCESS $TRATEGY
TO CONQUER INVESTING MISTAKE# 17:

Create a selling strategy prior to actually purchasing any investment. Know in advance when you will sell a stock that rises, and when you will dump an investment that is tanking.

18
MISTAKE

FAILING TO STICK WITH YOUR SELL STRATEGY

Frank Owen, the head of FR Owen & Associates in Charlotte, North Carolina, has been in business for nearly 25 years. He has 1,500 clients, most of them schoolteachers who work with kindergarten to 12th grade students. Like the bulk of the American public, these busy teachers "are not illiterate, but they are financially uninformed," says Owen.

Many of Owen's clients need help planning for retirement. For some, that means planning 30 years into the future. As a result, Owen tries to get his clients to think long-term.

For many investors who sell at the wrong time, Owen says it's because they're looking in the rear view mirror. "They need to focus on what's going to happen instead of what has happened," he says.

Owen also believes it's human nature to get scared about investing. Even for those people who do have a plan, "they tend to forget it when times get tough. That's partially the fault of the client, but also of the advisor who may not communicate regularly about the plan," Owen says.

"GUT INSTINCTS" ARE NO STRATEGY

It might be tempting to hang onto a losing investment because your "gut instincts" tells you to, or based on later research you've done that makes you think that a poor-performing stock will rebound. It may, in fact, come back. But don't wait around for it. Stick with your established game plan for consistency, investment discipline and, ultimately, the best overall investment performance. This way you won't have to say, "I coulda, woulda, shoulda" later on.

Investors who abandon their established sell strategy become undisciplined, suffer inconsistent or poor portfolio performance, and are more likely to sell at the wrong time for the wrong reasons.

That's what Owen has frequently witnessed. He says he's seen highly impressive looking action plans, all done up nicely with pretty graphics and printed on laser paper. It's a nice package, but it's little more than window dressing if the advice isn't followed. "You can get as fancy as you want to be. But if you don't implement the plan, it's just words on a piece of paper," Owen says.

To help you stick with your selling strategy, I recommend that you ask yourself the following three questions before you get rid of an investment:

1. Are my actions in keeping with my pre-established sell criteria?

2. Has this investment ceased to serve my investment needs?

3. Do I have a better, alternative investment in mind into which I can quickly place my money?

If the answers to all three questions are "YES," that's a good candidate to be sold from your portfolio.

Whatever happens, don't reverse course mid-way through your investing game plan and try to alter your selling game plan just to fit one individual stock that you don't want to sell. Neither should you get "trigger happy" just because the market falls unexpectedly. As long as your stop-loss limit hasn't been reached, or as long as the reason you bought a stock or a fund remains valid, you should probably hang onto that stock. Otherwise, you're defeating the whole purpose of having a written sell strategy. It's a guide that will improve your investing results with discipline and consistency.

$UMMARY $UCCESS $TRATEGY

TO CONQUER INVESTING MISTAKE #18:

Stick to your sell strategy. Don't abandon your game plan. Use stop-loss orders, and keep your strategy in black-and-white before you to remind you of your plans. Only sell, both winning and losing investments, according to your pre-set selling criteria.

19
MISTAKE

LETTING YOUR EMOTIONS RULE
YOUR DECISION-MAKING PROCESS

One of the best things about the human body is that it works so marvelously – and when it doesn't, it gives us messages that something has gone afoul. When your body gets overworked, for example, you feel tired and a little achy – some signs that you need to take it easy. More serious aches and pains or chronic fatigue are your signals that perhaps you should go see a doctor. In short, when something is wrong with your body, you literally get a "bad feeling." Maybe that's why physicians use the word "disease" (translate: dis-ease) to describe the ailment or discomfort sick patients feel.

If only investing was that simple.

When investors get a pain in their gut – or any kind of "gut feeling" at all – more often than not heeding that feeling brings disaster, not relief. The reason? Acting on a "gut feeling" means you're letting your emotions guide your decision-making process. When this happens, you inevitably make poor choices, experts agree.

Want to know one of the most common "gut feelings" that emotion-wracked investors experience? It's the strong yet unfounded belief that a downtrodden stock will miraculously rebound and come back from some precipitous decline. But "most investors, I'm afraid, have a pretty slap-dash idea of what a stock's upside is," Harvard University finance professor Samuel Hayes once told me. He says part of the reason for investors' unrealistic expectations about a stock's future performance is that people get stuck thinking about the company's price history – something that has no bearing on how well the company will perform in the future.

If you're among those investors saying: "I'll sell when the stock comes back," just remember that any investment that has lost 50% of its value has to climb 100% to get back to break-even status. That's a tall order in any market condition.

Donn Sharer, a former vice president of financial services at MetLife, has an interesting hypothesis about what happens to people who buy stocks, and then watch their investments go down the tubes. In a nutshell, his theory is that people who lose money in the stock market go through stages not unlike individuals coming to grips with the death of a family member or loved one.

"It kind of mirrors the grieving process: there's denial, sadness, anger — all those emotions," Sharer theorizes. Sharer is no psychologist. But he may be on to something when it comes to the way investors behave when faced with a blow to their pocketbooks.

Experts long ago discovered that putting money at risk – and especially selling an investment – brings to the surface an array of emotional issues for investors. Ironically, you're just as likely to experience emotional bouts over selling winning investments as you are about selling losing ones. But those emotions must be overcome.

When emotions dictate your investing decisions, faulty judgment kicks in, impulsive behavior often emerges, and financial losses result. Being guided by emotions also leads to heightened anxiety about the investing process, sleepless nights, and obsessing over investments.

Greed and fear are two of the most dominant emotions you have to guard against. "There really is even a physiological issue surrounding fear, especially fear of loss. Fear is centered out of the brain stem, so it's very primal and much more intense," says Deanna Tillisch of Northwestern Mutual.

Feelings of loyalty, guilt and sentimentality are other common emotional barriers that get in the way of making smart selling decisions. Perhaps you inherited a stock from a parent or grandparent and feel obligated to keep it. Some investors hang onto losing stock because they don't want to hurt the feelings of their broker or their spouse who recommended it. Or maybe you work for a large company where everyone else buys company stock, so you fall in step – even though the investment doesn't suit your needs. Or maybe you *used* to work for the company and holding onto those shares makes you feel as if you're still "a part of the team" at your former employer.

No matter what, though, emotions have no role in your investment portfolio.

Needless to say, there's no magic wand, good luck charm or special pill you can take to get those emotions in check. (That's probably for the best, since such a thing would foster its own set of investment mistakes … as if we don't have enough issues to tackle!)

The best way to conquer your emotions while investing is to have a sell strategy, as described in Chapter 17. But there are some other things you can do to overcome the numerous and inevitable emotions that bubble up during the investing process.

DO YOU NEED PROFESSIONAL HELP?

One obvious solution is to hire a professional to take over the selling decisions for you. This may be absolutely necessary if you're one of those people who not only "falls in love with" an investment, but also "gets married" to it, blinded by it, and starts to believe the investment can do no wrong! If this scenario accurately describes you, divorce yourself from the process by retaining the services of a trustworthy, competent money manager. It may take some getting used to at first. But in the long run, you'll be glad you made the switch.

THE BUDDY SYSTEM

For those of you who bristle at the thought of paying a professional advisor and letting that person call the shots, another option is to enlist the help of a friend as an investment partner. That was an idea once suggested to me by Rishi Narang, then president and vice chairman of Tradeworx, a New York financial analytics firm. "When you have a trading partner, you tell each other what your plan is and the other guy's job is to hold you to it," said Narang, who uses this method with a pal he's known for a dozen years.

It's a good thing he adopted the buddy system, too, because Narang was married in July 2002. Before the "Big Day," he actively bought and sold stocks in a trading account he established to help pay for the wedding. But he always knew that his wife "would kill me if I lost too much money," Narang said jokingly. On a more serious note, any stock in that wedding-fund account that fell 5% immediately got sold because of a 5% stop-loss rule to which Narang adheres.

Occasionally, though, when a stock declines 5%, Narang doesn't want to cut bait. That's when his trading buddy steps in. "He tells me what I already know," Narang said, which is to unload the stock immediately, in accordance with his plan. Having a trading partner "makes a huge difference," according to Narang. "It's the same thing as having a spotter or a coach."

If you think you could benefit from a black-and-white reminder about your sell strategy — but not necessarily another person's involvement — an "investment policy statement" may be in order. "It's just a

> guiding document that articulates the specific goals
> of your investment plan, how much risk is accept-
> able, and the range of what you can invest in any as-
> set class," explains Robert Wolfe, a CERTIFIED FINANCIAL
> PLANNER™ practitioner at Capital Planning Group in
> Fort Lauderdale, Fla.

In years past, only very wealthy individuals, families and pension plans used investment policy statements. Nowadays, smart investors in all income-brackets create their own investment policy statements. Wolfe uses them with all his clients because they "help take emotion out of the mix." As a financial advisor, "You have to be half technician and half psychologist these days," he believes.

A final strategy for dealing with the emotional roller coaster that investing throws us all on is to track your behavior in hopes of improving it.

Richard Geist is president of the Newton, Mass.-based Institute of Psychology and Investing, which researches the psychological aspects of financial decision-making.

Geist says that people "tend to make the same mistakes over and over."

"It may be helpful to write down what happened around the mistakes," counsels Geist, who is also a clinical instructor in the department of psychiatry at Harvard Medical School. "A few months later people often see a pattern," in their decision-making, he adds.

Geist figures that once people recognize how and why their faulty logic or poor judgment creeps in, they can begin to reverse those trends and become better investors.

Don't be guided by greed, fear of loss, sentimentality, guilt or any other emotion. The best antidote to these powerful emotions is having a sell strategy (See advice in Chapter 17). But you can also enlist the help of an investing buddy to help you stick to your investment game plan. Some people may have to hire a pro, and turn over to that person the responsibility of deciding when to sell various investments. This is advisable if you can't divorce yourself from the investing process because you find yourself "getting married" to a stock, bond or other investment.

It's also helpful to formulate an "investment policy statement," a black-and-white reminder of how you're supposed to be investing, what you're supposed to be investing in and under what circumstances you should sell.

Whatever you do, make a promise to yourself that from this day forward you will no longer base your sell decisions on impulses, hunches, or other emotional whims. Just remember that listening to your body is a great rule of thumb in medicine. But in investing, relying on that "gut feeling" can be hazardous to your wealth – a situation that just may cause you to really bust a gut.

$UMMARY $UCCESS $TRATEGY

TO CONQUER INVESTING MISTAKE #19:

Let your head, not your emotions, rule your decision-making process. Try to keep fear and greed in check. They can cause you to make irrational decisions.

20
MISTAKE

REFUSING TO ADMIT YOU MADE
A MISTAKE AND TO MOVE ON

Investors too stubborn to admit their mistakes often suffer the steepest losses of all. They hang onto losing investments for far too long, they stick with failing companies even as they fall into bankruptcy, and they throw off their asset allocation strategy. These investors may also adopt a demoralized, defeatist attitude about investing.

Does this sound like you?

If so, you've got to change your outlook.

Don't be stubborn. Cut your losses by using trigger points to sell declining securities. And forget about trying to "break even" on every single investment. Remember that savvy investors consider first their overall portfolio's performance. They focus on absolute returns. Then they worry about the individual stocks, bonds and other components. Finally, smart investors don't always make up their losses in the same place they got them. They "break even" by selling losing investments and replacing them with better-performing ones.

I remember one investor from Maryland I once interviewed. This retired gentleman refused to sell a stock, Plantronics, and had suffered big losses in the process. He bought the stock for around $50 a share in early 2000. A year later, it had fallen to $16. Headquartered in Santa Cruz, Calif., Plantronics makes earphone pieces and telephone headsets. As of June 2003, the stock changed hands for around $22. This investor thought his investment would be a sure winner. But he later came to think of it, in his words, as a "dog" in his portfolio. Still, he never sold the stock. He said he was waiting for the market to turn around and "validate" his belief in Plantronics.

I'm certainly not suggesting that Plantronics won't turn around. (This is, after all the company that made the headset that astronaut Neil Armstrong used to broadcast his famous "One small step for man" transmission from the moon in the 1969. And today, Plantronics is a leader in supplying hands-free devices for cell phones, something a growing number of states are requiring of drivers nationwide). What I am asserting though, is that this gentleman bought the stock with expectations of getting immediate double-digit growth. And three years later, that still hadn't happened.

"If you have cancer in an arm, you cut it out to save the rest of the body," reasons money manager and hedge fund expert Daniel Strachman. "The problem is, most investors don't want to do that."

Sometimes it can be tough to reverse course and change directions. Have you ever been in a car with a driver who was clearly lost, but he or she refused to stop and ask for directions? Just like that person could soon get back on the right road with a little proper guidance, so too could investors who make a u-turn when they realize they've gone the wrong way.

TAKE SOME SOLACE

If you are willing to sell your losers, at least you might take some solace in getting out of a losing position the right way. Nick Hodges, the CPA from Fullerton, CA, recommends carrying forward your loss for up to 15 years, as the law allows, or using it to offset capital gains.

Some people "also have real estate," he notes. "Offset those gains with stock losses," he advises.

You should also realize that it's O.K. to admit your investing mistakes – they will happen. The more important thing is: what are you doing to do about them? That's where your mettle as a serious and savvy investor gets tested.

"Everybody wants to talk about what they did right. You know, the cocktail party chatter where people claim to have made brilliant investments," says David Winters, chairman of the Mutual Series Funds. "But most people are never straight enough to say 'Hey, I did this wrong.'"

Not so for Winters, who makes a point to disclose to shareholders what went right – and wrong – in any given year.

Asked about investing mistakes he's made, Winters said: "We're cheapskates, and sometimes we've not been willing to pay up for stocks." As a result, he added, some good prospects "have gotten away from us."

But with the Mutual Series Funds' international funds posting three and five-year returns of 8-9%, most of the firm's shareholders are no doubt pleased with their overall results.

$UMMARY $UCCESS $TRATEGY

TO CONQUER INVESTING MISTAKE #20:

Admit your mistakes and move on. Don't waste time and money on investments that are clearly money-losing propositions. And don't justify hanging onto a sour investment by saying "I'll sell when it comes back." Some quick math: any stock that falls 50% must then rise 100% to break even.

21

MISSING OPPORTUNITIES
TO TAKE PROFITS

Investors who neglect to book their gains at the correct time rank among the most anguished of investors. In the bull market, many of these people owned stocks that generated tremendous profits. But these investors never saw one penny of those gains. It was sort of like they won the lottery jackpot, but wouldn't cash in their winning ticket. Worse still, some investors held out for even bigger gains only to watch their investments turn sour, resulting in financial losses.

Avoid the temptation to be greedy. Sell when you reach a pre-established target. For example, your investment has doubled or you've reached a required dollar amount for a specific goal such as saving for your kid's college education.

Realize that booking gains is part of adhering to a winning investment strategy. So don't fret too much over the prospect that you "might miss out" on future gains. Rather, look at selling opportunities where you've made a profit as indications that you are meeting your personal and financial objectives.

And remember the advice of financial expert Denis Walsh, of Money Concepts. Most of his clients are people in their 40s and 50s. They've often left a job or are between jobs. They're seeking help with their 401(k) because they've never had such a big chunk of money to invest for themselves.

The thing he sees happening is that some stocks perform almost "too well." By that, he explains: "It's almost automatic that if you have four or five types of investments, and one of them outperforms the market, (clients) will be resistant to taking some of those monies and moving it elsewhere."

In fact the investor's automatic reaction will be to put more money into the one fund that did well, according to Walsh. So he find himself fighting the client's urge to "go with something that's great."

At the same time, he has to explain to the client that the *more* a stock vastly outperforms the market or its industry, the *less* likely it is that such out-performance will continue in the future. So like many advisors, a big part of Walsh's job is educational. Money Concepts has 750 representatives around the country – – as well as affiliates in Ireland, Canada, New Zealand, and 40 regional offices. CPAs and tax professionals run about one-third of these offices. CERTIFIED FINANCIAL PLANNER™ professionals and other financial specialists head the rest.

TAKE THE MONEY AND RUN!

Even when investors sell for a sizeable profit, however, they sometimes second guess themselves. That was the case with Lara Oyetunde, who initially considered herself a "very conservative" investor.

For Oyetunde, that entailed being properly diversified, buying only mutual funds, and investing for the long-term. But amid the Internet craze of 1999, Oyetunde became intrigued by the possibility of making much bigger profits with individual stocks. So that summer, she dove into the equities market, buying shares of Intel for $57.25 apiece and Yahoo for $159 a share.

For several months thereafter, Yahoo traded all over the place, wreaking havoc on Oyetunde's nerves. "It was kind of fun, but definitely nerve-wracking," she said of the experience. She ultimately sold Yahoo for $184 a share. And by November 1999, she let her Intel shares go for $79.95 each. When Yahoo later shot up to about $205, Oyetunde regretted her decision. She said she was just getting comfortable with trusting her investing instincts but "panicked" and sold too early.

In hindsight, she likely made the right choice given the bear market that was to come beginning in early 2000.

$UMMARY $UCCESS $TRATEGY

TO CONQUER INVESTING MISTAKE #21:

Take your profits when the opportunity arises. Again, don't be greedy. Nor should you take money off the table prematurely. Use your sell strategy as a guide.

22
MISTAKE

EXCESSIVE TRADING

I know some people who visit the mall practically every other day – and then these shopaholics wonder why their credit card bills are so high. The same could be said for some investors. They engage in a form of shopping excess as well, in this case excessive trading of stocks, mutual funds, or other investments.

But trading too frequently leads to a number of problems: the generation of high commissions, short-term capital gains taxes, and portfolio under-performance.

To avoid this mistake, buy only well-researched securities. Buy only when you can truly afford it. Avoid getting a margin loan just because you're itching to get in on a "once in lifetime" deal. Buy only after you've carefully considered the risks involved; and buy only when you're positive the investment complements your existing portfolio and doesn't duplicate some holdings you already own. On the back end, sell only as per your pre-designed sell strategy. That's the best way to avoid excessive trading.

If you won't take my word for it, consider the story of a former day-trader I know who traded at the height of the Internet bubble. She had been a successful stockbroker at a major Wall Street brokerage before she took $50,000 of her money to begin full-time day-trading in 1998. She quickly learned how active trading resulted in stiff fees. By the time she stopped trading, she'd lost $18,630. Of that total, $15,040 was in commissions and execution expenses.

RESEARCH ON TRADING AND GENDER

University of California professor Terrance Odean also says over-trading affects the testosterone laden (that's you men out there!) more than the feminine sex. According to Odean's research, men trade 45% more actively than do women. Single men traded 67% more actively than single women. As a result, single women fared better performance wise – some 2.3 percentage points better per year over single men. Overall, women got better returns than men, 1.4 percentage points higher, according to Odean's research.

His findings were drawn from a study that Odean and another colleague did in which they examined 150,000 accounts from a discount broker and studied the trading patterns from 1991 through 1997. They found that on average, women achieve better returns than do men because women trade less often.

Odean also discovered that online trading has, predictably, led to people trading more frequently. In 1998, the number of online brokerage accounts stood at roughly 5 million. As of 2003, that figure quadrupled to an estimated 20.4 million online accounts, managing more than $3 trillion online, according to Forrester Research.

USE THE WEB THE RIGHT WAY

No one is suggesting that you stop any online trading in which you might engage. In fact, the web can be a tremendously valuable place to learn, educate yourself about investing, and cut costs too.

But since it's faster, easier and cheaper to trade online (and more thrilling as well, some investors say), just realize that you may be tempted to do a bit more armchair trading than is wise. For most people, the temptation to over-trade won't be too hard to resist because of their busy schedules and a million other matters to which they must attend. Perhaps that's why, according to Odean's research, it's the single crowd, especially unmarried males, that are most likely to spend excessive time at the computer screen trading.

Portfolio turnover rates are also very telling. Women tend to turnover their portfolio an average of 53% a year, while men did it at a rate of 77% a year. Part of Odean's research showed that people had been beating the market by about 2 percentage points a year before they moved online. And once they started online trading, they typically under-performed the market by more than 3 percentage points.

THE ONLINE TRADING BOOM

There are roughly 100 online brokerage firms in the U.S. with millions customer accounts, according to Gomez Advisors, a Concord, Mass., consulting firm. Professional day traders, however, number between 3,500 and 4,000 people nationwide, according to industry estimates. (Of course, this doesn't include traders who work for brokerage firms).

The head of a major day-trading group also once said that the vast majority of day traders lose money during their first four to six months. The losses typically range from $10,000 to $50,000.

In January 1999, Momentum Securities Management Co., one of the largest professional day trading firms in the U.S. released a survey about day-trading performance. The three month survey, which collected data from 107 traders in Momentum's six Texas offices, revealed that 58% of newcomers lost an average of $21,479. On a brighter note, nearly two-thirds of traders who got past a three-to-five month "learning curve" made an average of $28,426, the study said.

Critics of the survey argued that it didn't disclose how many traders actually made it through that initial three-month period. And some regulators say at least 80% of day traders lose money.

As a reminder, for most of you, adopt a long-term strategy to guide you through the investing process. Blow-by-blow trading in the markets should be reserved for only the most sophisticated of investors, people who trade for a living.

> ### $UMMARY $UCCESS $TRATEGY
> ### TO CONQUER INVESTING MISTAKE #22:
>
> Trade less frequently. People who over-trade tend to make poor investment decisions and invest impulsively. Excessive trading can also frequently cause you to pay more commissions and more taxes to Uncle Sam.

23
MISTAKE

NOT TAKING TAXES INTO CONSIDERATION

The next chapter in this book will look at investors who place too much emphasis on taxes. At the other end of the spectrum are investors who give no thought whatsoever to taxes. This, too, is a mistake. Investors who don't take taxes into consideration wind up paying the government more taxes than necessary. They could have often saved a bundle with just a bit of planning or a little more patience.

Look at the pre- and post-tax ramifications of any investment decision: whether that decision is to buy, hold or sell. Recognize the benefits of paying long-term capital gains taxes, which currently top out at 20%. By contrast, depending on an investor's tax bracket, short-term gains can be taxed at a rate of nearly 40%, notes Lehman Brothers tax expert Robert Willens.

It may sound silly to say this, but one thing you should consider – especially if you plan to sell a large chunk of stock — is whether or not you'll actually have the money to pay any large tax bill. You don't want to get a big surprise from the government after April 15th.

CPA Nick Hodges can tick off a litany of tax mistakes he's seen investors make.

One of the biggies, according to Hodges, is not having any year-end planning with your financial intermediaries, in order to coordinate year-end stock sales and harvest the appropriate losses. It doesn't matter if you've not been diligent enough to do this in the past, or if your broker or planner hasn't been diligent enough in doing so, the fact remains: from now on, you're going to be responsible for making sure it gets done.

Hodges also sees some people who refuse to sell individual stock positions for fear of paying capital gains taxes. So what happens? The person rides the stock all the way down. They do avoid paying capital gains, but they also eliminated all the profits that could've helped pay those capital gains. For example, say you bought 500 shares of a stock at $35 a share, and one year later it rose to $56. With a proper sell strategy, after a 60% run-up you would probably be inclined to sell some of this stock and lock in your profits. But what if you didn't just because you didn't want to pay taxes? Well, now let's assume that your stock started to fall – and fall sharply. If it dropped back down to $35, you've lost a gross profit of $10,500 (500 shares X $21 a share price increase). If you paid a 20% capital gains tax on that $10,500, you'd give up $2,100 and keep $8,400. But by failing to sell, and watching the stock crash back to $35, you lose all your profit. Even worse, if the stock goes down to, say $22, you've incurred a loss.

Now which is better: to lose money, to "break even" or to net an $8,400 profit? Look at it this way: By taking your profits at the prudent time, you effectively use the gains you generate to pay the requisite taxes.

Another example of a tax-related investing mistake, as mentioned earlier in Chapter 7, is putting the right investments in the wrong accounts. Hodges knew of a fund in which there were over $300,000 worth of tax-exempt bonds inside of Individual Retirement Accounts. Again, the investors effectively took tax-free income and turned it into taxable income. Here's a brief example of a retirement-related investing mistake that occurred when the investor didn't properly consider tax consequences.

IN THEIR OWN WORDS: INVESTORS SHARE LESSONS LEARNED

> My biggest investing error was converting my Individual Retirement Account to a Roth IRA at the very height of the market. That meant I paid taxes for four years on its highest-ever value, while it fell to half that amount in that time.
>
> John Voelcker

MUTUAL FUND RELATED TAX ERRORS

Have you ever erred in exchanging from one mutual fund to another fund within the same fund family? Unbeknownst to you, this exchange could create an unexpected capital gains tax when you think it's a tax-free exchange. So be careful here.

A final blunder: don't make the mistake of viewing your IRA as your short-term piggy bank. You probably know that you can get a tax deduction, subject to income limitations, on money you put into a regular IRA account. But what happens if you deposit money you can't really afford – just so you can save taxes? If you make a contribution you can't truly afford, you'll later likely tap the account, get hit with a 10% penalty, as well as have to pay ordinary income rates on the funds you withdrew.

$UMMARY $UCCESS $TRATEGY

TO CONQUER INVESTING MISTAKE #23:

Consider the tax implications of any selling decision. Ideally, you should hold a security more than
12 months to get favorable capital gains treatment.
Any capital investment you own for less than 12
months is taxed at ordinary income rates, which are
usually much higher.

24
MISTAKE

WORRYING TOO MUCH ABOUT TAXES

Is there any one out there who relishes paying taxes?

If so, I don't know him. The one blessing about paying taxes, of course, is the fact that since you owe them, that means there was some income on which to base those taxes. That's a plus. Besides that, however, I'm going to assume most of you are like me: you want to pay the least amount of taxes that is possible – and legal, of course!

If you are a high net worth individual, or if you own stock options, and you want more information about increasing your after-tax returns, a wonderful web site to use is *www.myStockOptions.com*. Run by Bruce Brumberg, a stock options expert who also has a background in securities law, myStockOptions.com offers you all the ins and outs of the tax ramifications of owning, holding or excercising incentive stock options and Non-qualified stock options.

One of the key messages consistently delivered by Brumberg, and the experts who write for his site, is that taxes should not drive your decisions. Ever.

To make the best buy, hold and selling decisions, you must first consider whether the investment makes solid financial sense – in terms of potential performance, risk to you, and so forth. Tax considerations, while very important, should nevertheless come second.

But this is one of those rules that no matter how many times you try to drive the message home to investors, many people simply won't listen. Please don't make that mistake.

Countless investors hang onto to stocks they should sell because of a fear of paying taxes. But this flawed thinking makes investors own the wrong investments for far too long. In many cases where a stock subsequently falls in value, investors would have been better off simply making whatever tax payments were due.

Don't let the tax tail wag the dog. First pick the most prudent investment strategy and individual investments. Then weigh the tax implications. In the long run, the returns you get from making good investment choices will outweigh any money you must fork over to Uncle Sam.

STRATEGIC IDEAS TO CUT TAXES

From a strategic standpoint, it's also a good idea to think about how to get the best after-tax returns from the investments you buy in the future.

Many experts think that the May 2003 tax cut passed by Congress on dividends will make dividend-paying stocks more attractive. Don't, however, expect the tax cut to juice up your near-term returns. Instead, the long-term (and more lasting) benefit to you will likely occur if publicly-traded companies start to increase their dividends. If that happens, those dividend-paying stocks will be highly sought after, especially since for years dividends have been getting slashed or eliminated altogether a few more ideas:

- You can get Standard & Poor's Earnings and Dividend Rankings on more than 3,400 U.S. companies through Standard & Poor's Stock Reports. S&P says the information is available through the 120,000 investment advisors and brokers that subscribe to Stock Reports, as well as through investor web sites sponsored by brokerage firms.

- Also, check out the American Association of Individual Investors' Guide to Dividend Reinvestment Plans. AAII members receive the guide free of charge each June. The publication explains how you can use the dividend reinvestment programs of hundreds of companies to buy additional stock at no commission. AAII is an independent, non-profit corporation formed in 1978. Its mission is to help individual investors learn to manage their own assets through education, research and information.

- Another strategy to consider is buying iShares, which have become tremendously popular. The reason investors like them is because they're good at reducing taxes and cutting costs. There are nearly 80 iShares funds segmented by sector, country, market cap, or investing style. For more information, call 800-iSHARES or log onto the web at *www.iShares.com*. iShares are offered through Barclays Global Investors.

- Add municipal bonds to your portfolio if you don't already own some. They are free from federal taxes, and in many parts of the country they are also exempt from state taxes. High net worth individuals, in particular, should have municipal bonds in their portfolios for tax-reduction purposes.

- A handful of companies now offer online services to help investors easily figure out the tax consequences of their investment choices. NetWorthStrategies.com of Bend, Oregon, which sells a product call StockOpter, is one such business. Dynamic Capital Management of Anchorage, Alaska is another. The latter company, owned by money manager David Gottstein, has a patented system called DynamicTaxOptimizer that helps investors figure out the best time to sell a stock or book losses for tax purposes.

One other tip: Some tax averse investors may be considering borrowing money from your broker (getting a margin loan) in order to exercise and hold onto stock options. Here's a word to the wise: Don't do it. In most cases you're better off using other funds.

$UMMARY $UCCESS $TRATEGY

TO CONQUER INVESTING MISTAKE #24:

Don't worry too much about taxes. Take taxes into account; but they shouldn't be the driving force behind your decisions. Any investment you buy or sell should make economic and rational investment sense first. Tax considerations are secondary.

PART V

FINANCIAL ADVISOR FOUL-UPS

25

MISTAKE

OMITTING INDEPENDENT RESEARCH

We all know someone who loves to have designer clothing or brand name goods. Some people are lured by advertising come-ons. Other consumers have a desire to "keep up with the Joneses." For whatever reason, many of these individuals wouldn't dream of shopping at retail outlets where they can't purchase items that don't have a recognized label of some sort.

Interestingly, this "bigger is better" kind of thinking seems to extend from Main Street to Wall Street. Many investors who are looking for financial research, information and advice also automatically flock to the biggest, most well-known investment firms and brokerages. In most cases, these institutions have been around for many decades and are household names.

As a rule of thumb, it certainly is good practice to consider doing business with established institutions from any industry. After all, you have to figure that if a company has been around 50 years or more, it's probably been doing something right. But the problem with this logic in the financial services world is that all too often many investors have an automatic tendency to seek counsel, products and services *only* from the major Wall Street players. In particular, some investors rely solely on Wall Street research, while completely disregarding (often to their detriment) independent financial services firms that also have a lot to offer.

Think about your own situation for a minute. Whom do you rely on for investment research? For many of you, the answer will be that you are using a big Wall Street outfit, a company known in the industry as a "bulge bracket" firm.

If this describes you, I want you to think about other options available to you. My goal here is not to make you yank all your money from the investment firm where you accounts are now held or to not buy research from that firm. Rather, I simply want to you to be aware of the dangers of relying on any single source of information. Moreover, I want you to discover the tremendous benefits of using independent research. And finally, I want you to realize that while many independent research shops may be "off brand" names, and not familiar to you, this doesn't make then second-rate in terms of quality. In fact, many of them regularly produce research that rivals their larger peers.

I believe that depending too heavily on Wall Street analysts, even well-known ones, can sometimes cause the average investor to buy an investment – and especially to sell it – at the wrong time. It can also lead to an individual purchasing inappropriate securities that don't meet their needs. Investors who rely unduly on Wall Street pros are often simply following the pack, and jumping in too late on supposedly "good" investments.

To avoid these mistakes, here are some key points to keep in mind.

- **Be discriminating in how you view research.**

   In general, look critically at Wall Street research when the firm has an investment banking relationship with the company it is covering. In an ideal world, there is supposed to be a "Chinese Wall" that separates the investment banking side of a brokerage firm's operations from its research division. In reality, however, this is sometimes not the case. And critics say some brokerages may not be as critical of companies they cover, when the brokerage firm wants to underwrite initial public offerings (IPOs) or do mergers and acquisition work, and other advisory services for that corporation. A 2002 BusinessWeek cover story, dubbed "The Investor Betrayed," cited research conflicts of interest and several Wall Street scandals as reasons why investors no longer trusted many brokerages. Indeed, as of June 2003, investors had won a proposed $1 billion settlement from 309 companies that issued IPOs in the late 1990s. These companies, mainly telecommunications companies and Internet businesses, were widely touted by Wall Street analysts.

- **Know how to really interpret Wall Street research**

  Only 1% of all analyst recommendations are sell ratings, according to First Call, which tracks corporate earnings. Logic alone tells you that of all the thousands of publicly-traded companies that are rated by analysts, way more than 1% of them should be considered "sell" candidates. So understand that many Wall Street ratings are inflated, according to Chuck Hill, research chief at First Call. Thus, "strong buy" means buy the stock, "buy" means "hold," and "hold" really means "sell," says Hill.

- **If you have the time and desire, do much of your own due diligence.**

  Otherwise, pay a trusted broker, financial planner or advisor. Develop a relationship with that person - and hold him or her accountable for investing recommendations. (For more information on how to do that, see Chapter 27).

Also, if you do start to seriously do your own research, keep in mind the following list of "red flags" in company announcements, quarterly corporate earnings reports, or any SEC filings:

- a "going concern" notation from an auditor
- big drops in revenues or profits
- lawsuits that could potentially be very costly
- wholesale management shake-ups

ANALYSTS REMAIN OPTIMISTIC

A *Wall Street Journal* article from February 2003 noted that most Wall Street analysts remained unshaken in their unbridled optimism about stocks. In short, most of the analysts rating stocks offered the belief that those companies would post above-average, double-digit growth over the next several years. These predictions fly in the face of the fact that corporate earnings historically grow at about the same rate as the overall economy over time. And 10%-plus growth is nowhere on the radar screen for the U.S. economy in the near future. Still, analysts expected 345 companies in the S&P 500 Index to boost their earnings by more than 10% a year during the next three to five years. Another 123 companies were seen growing their earnings by more than 15%.

It would be great if these forecasts came true. But it seems like a long-shot that this will happen for many of these companies. Again, I'm not suggesting that analysts have no clue in their forecasts. As a note, for instance, soon after the *Wall Street Journal* article, stock prices surged tremendously. After hitting it's low on March 11, 2003 the market staged a three-month rally, with the Dow Jones Industrial Average rising 21%, the S&P 500 adding 23%, and the technology-heavy Nasdaq gaining 28%. It remains to be seen though, if corporate earnings will follow suit.

EXISTING INDEPENDENT SOURCES

If you want independent research today, it's actually plentiful to find. One major player that is widely respected is Standard & Poor's. Most investors think of S&P in the fixed-income arena. You probably know that S&P rates bonds, assigning some as investment grade securities, others as "junk" bonds, and so forth. But did you also know that S&P is an extremely established and trusted source of stock-research information for institutional investors? Pension funds and mutual fund managers in particular often turn to S&P and its sizeable equity research division.

S&P's stock pickers have done very well in making market calls – even in down markets. For instance, in 2001 S&P's stock picks posted gains of 22%. Meanwhile, the Dow lost 7%, the S&P 500 Index fell 11%, and the Nasdaq dropped 13%. You can use S&P's stock rating system, called STARS, which is found on the company's web site. During an interview, S&P equity research chief Ken Shea once told me: "We really pride ourselves on our independence, and the fact that S&P has been around for over 100 years. This is no fly by night operation."

Value Line is another trusted source of quality financial research. It too fiercely guards its status as an independent venue from which investors can get unbiased information. Once, when I was doing a story on this subject, Value Line research chief Stephen Sanborn said: "We don't have any investment banking relationships. We don't do corporate business. And we don't even let our analysts buy or sell stocks that they follow." Maybe that's why no less than billionaire Warren Buffett and Peter Lynch, of Fidelity fame, have both espoused the value of Value Line's research.

Weiss Ratings Inc. is a third solid source of independent research. The firm offers what it calls "financial safety ratings" on insurance companies, HMOs, banks and mutual funds.

RATING INDEPENDENT RESEARCH

By now, some of you may be saying: Oh, sure there's independent research out there, but how good is it? Excellent question. The answer is: much of it is very good – if you know where to turn. Like anything else, of course, you have independent firms with outstanding track records, such as Argus Research, and other ones with mediocre results. But according to one source, Investars, four of the five top research firms are independent companies.

Here are the three other ways to get information about independent research – and to compare it to research from traditional Wall Street firms.

- Go to *www.investars.com*.

  Investars is run by Kei Kianpoor, who's told me during several interviews in recent times that the value his firm offers is that it tells you how your portfolio would've performed if you followed a given firm's recommendations. Investars assesses both Wall Street and independent research firms' results.

  Regarding independent research entities, Investars has given high marks to Best Independent Research LLC. Best, founded in December 2002, is a consortium of five independent equities research firms. BIR member firms are Callard Research, LLC (Chicago, IL), Channel Trend (Dallas, TX), Columbine Capital Services (Colorado Springs, CO), Ford Equity Research (San Diego, CA), Global Capital Institute (managing partner - Chicago, IL), and Market Profile Theorems (Seattle, WA). As of 2003, these firms were among the top of Investars' one-year, two-year and three-year rankings by stock, industry and total portfolio.

  If you contact some of these firms to get their research, be prepared for sticker shock: many of them have very pricey research.

- Use *www.bnyjaywalk.com*. Jaywalk is a division of the Bank of New York that also offers good independent research and information. It's primarily geared toward institutional investors, so you can probably most readily access it through a broker or financial advisor that receives BNY Jaywalk's research.

- Subscribe to the Hulbert Financial Digest (*www.hulbertdigest.com*) for the most comprehensive information anywhere about investment newsletters that offer independent research. The publication, now a service of CBS MarketWatch, is run by Mark Hulbert. Hulbert follows 160 investment newsletters and the 500+ portfolios they recommend.

THE FUTURE OF INDEPENDENT RESEARCH

Here's another reason you should start to take independent research much more seriously: chances are you're going to be getting it one way or another. According to John Meserve, the president of BNY Jaywalk, his company has well over 1,000 clients and business grew 20% in 2002.

Wall Street firms are also recognizing that investors want independent research.

In March 2003, CSFB – a unit of Credit Suisse Group – was reportedly exploring launching an independent stock-research company under the name DLJ Research. DLJ stands for Donaldson, Lufkin & Jenrette, a company that Credit Suisse First Boston bought in the year 2000.

But in June 2003, CSFB squashed plans to launch that independent research operation. Still, according to the $1.4 billion Wall Street settlement involving 10 major investment dealers and banks, the firms are required to contract with at least three independent research providers and make available to clients that research, as well as their own research for five years.

$UMMARY $UCCESS $TRATEGY

TO CONQUER INVESTING MISTAKE #25:

Don't rely solely on Wall Street analysts. Independent research is often of very high quality. And getting differing opinions can frequently give you valuable insights into potential investments.

26
MISTAKE

NEGLECTING TO CHECK YOUR BROKER
OR FINANCIAL PLANNER'S HISTORY

The three-year downturn in the stock market that began in 2000 convinced a lot of investors that it was time for help. As a result, many former do-it-yourselfers turned to stockbrokers, financial planners and others for investment advice. But even if you pulled off a miracle, and didn't get badly hurt during that period, having a financial advisor, or perhaps several advisors, can help you immensely. Conversely, if you have an unqualified advisor, that can hurt you tremendously, as you'll later see from reading one investor's troubles in this chapter.

Some data from the Investment Company Institute, the mutual fund industry trade group, reveals the extent to which investors these days rely on financial intermediaries.

According to the ICI's 2003 Fact Book, only 13% of the money in stock and bond funds has come directly from an individual retail investor. The remaining 87% of the money has passed through an intermediary, such as a CERTIFIED FINANCIAL PLANNER™ practitioner or stockbroker. (401(k) plans are also included in this total).

Other ICI data also reveal the extent to which people go to their financial advisors. According to the 2001 Profile of Mutual Fund

Shareholders, 69% of mutual fund owners either strongly agreed, or somewhat agreed, with the following statement:

"I tend to rely on the advice of a professional advisor when making fund purchase and sales decisions."

Summing up how investors probably feel, ICI spokesman John Collins puts it this way: "I'm fairly confident that I could make a decent vegetarian Indian meal. But I'm also inclined to go to a restaurant where it's already made, or where there are experts who cook that type of cuisine."

In his *Finish Rich Workbook*, best-selling author David Bach offers this insight:

> "Enlisting the help of a financial advisor is not a sign of laziness or weakness or ignorance. To the contrary, it's a the smart thing to do." He goes on to write: "Think about it. Rich people almost always work with financial professionals. In fact, they usually have teams of attorneys, accountants, and financial planners who help them make sure their money is working hard for them. According to one recent study, nine out of ten people with more than $100,000 to invest prefer to work with a financial advisor. This is something to keep in mind if you are not yet as rich as you want to be."

If you do turn your finances over to a professional, or simply want to get some input and perspective before you make your own investing decisions, it's crucial that you pick the right kind of financial advisor – and that you check out that person's credentials.

So many investors carelessly enlist the "help" of ill-qualified or unscrupulous financial advisors – advisors who later turn out to "help themselves" to the investors money, or who make decisions that are not in the best interest of their clients.

To avoid this scenario, and for other practical reasons that will be discussed in this chapter, it is crucial that you do your homework and investigate the background of any potential financial advisor.

By "investigate" I don't mean you're going to do a full-scale background check on the individual, trying to figure out if the person's ever got a speeding ticket or what his neighbors think of him. I simply mean you should assess the person's professional track record, education, work experience, and whether or not he or she is skilled in the area or areas in which you need help.

If you don't check out your financial advisor, that's like jumping into the shower before putting your hand in there to test the water temperature. You might get burned.

Sometimes, careful diligent research still won't unearth a con artist who is determined to scam you and other investors. After all, it's possible that a no-good advisor has yet to be busted for his or her wrongdoing, so there's no record of that fact. But at least you can have a weeding out process to eliminate potential advisors who do have major blemishes on their record, and are therefore clearly undesirable.

Investors who neglect to check out their advisor's history subject themselves to people who may be inexperienced, unprofessional, or unqualified. That was the case for one New Jersey investor who says she wound up with an incompetent advisor.

IN THEIR OWN WORDS:
INVESTORS SHARE LESSONS LEARNED

I listened to my daughter's advice to get a planner to help me invest about $10,000 wisely. The planner was a Wall Street advisor with hardly any experience and apparently not enough clients to keep his job. After I turned over my $10,000 to him, he lost his job

and had never completed some paperwork properly to have my money transferred from one fund to an account at his firm. Apparently, he was trying to transfer money from an IRA to a money market account and the system wouldn't allow it. To make the story short, it took 11 months to correct the problem. The money sat idle without gaining any interest. The matter has finally been resolved, but I had to pay fees to both firms during the entire period although my money was held up. The major lesson learned is to not go with just any planner referred to you. Many of them are clueless as to simple procedures of transferring funds.

Ida Spruell

Paterson, New Jersey

In extreme cases, an investor may hire someone with regulatory blotches on their record – a big red flag because the advisor may have mistreated other investors. Individuals who are ignorant about their broker or financial planner's background also sometimes lack confidence or trust in that advisor.

When you are in the market for a financial intermediary, here are some guidelines to follow:

- **Interview at least three prospects.** Ask for recommendations, then call those clients and ask what kind of service and advice they've received and whether or not they've been happy with the individual in question.

- **Ask for Parts 1 and 2 of the person's ADV form**, which discloses his or her professional regulatory history. Boston Globe personal finance columnist Charles Jaffe, the author of *The Right Way To Hire Financial Help*, has been quoted as saying the ADV form "is a complete deal breaker for me."

He said that if you ask a broker for the complete form, and he only sends Part 1, "I don't even need to check" Part 2.

- **Also consult the National Association of Securities Dealers** to learn a stockbroker's professional, educational and regulatory history, including whether the individual has been fined or sanctioned for wrongdoing. In addition to having a very good web site, *www.NASD.com*, the NASD maintains a Public Disclosure Information Center that you can call at 800-289-9999.

- If the person claims to be a CERTIFIED FINANCIAL PLANNER™ practitioner or a Chartered Financial Analyst, **call to the appropriate professional organizations** (the Certified Financial Planner Board of Standards and the Association for Investment Management and Research, respectively) to verify those credentials and make sure the person is in good standing.

- **Finally, you can contact your state securities agencies** via the North American Securities Administrators Association *(www.NASAA.org)* to get more information about individual brokers or brokerage firms with whom you might consider doing business.

In general, you want to hire someone who is skillful, sensitive to your needs, experienced, and communicative in a way that you like. For instance, if you strongly prefer to do business in person or by telephone, but the advisor indicates that he mainly deals with clients via e-mail, the two of you likely won't have the best chemistry and rapport. It's also enlightening to ask potential advisors about their "typical clients" and about how many clients they have whose situations are similar to yours. If you're a 33-year old single parent with a $35,000 a year income, it's probably not wise to hire an advisor who works almost exclusively with retired couples, or with business owners earning $250,000 annually.

COMMISSIONS VS. FLAT FEES

Whenever you hire a financial advisor, you also want to know how that individual will be paid. Most often, it will be on a commission basis, a flat-fee arrangement, or some combination thereof.

Frank Owen, the CFP® practitioner from F.R. Owen & Associates, says he tells his clients up front that he works on commission. At the same time, he says it's a misconception that "if someone is getting a commission they're just pushing a product and taking you to the cleaners." His advice on picking an advisor: "check their pedigree and make sure they have your interest at heart."

HIGH-TOUCH SERVICE

Let me offer you a case in point of such a financial advisor, an individual who is really earning his keep. The person is Kevin Albritton, the head of AFS, a financial services firm founded in January 1996. Not only is Albritton very-well credentialed – with MCRS, CLU, ChFC, and CFP® designations – but he makes a point to be involved in professional industry associations and to constantly challenge himself to learn and keep up with changing practices and ideas.

Best of all, however, is his approach to dealing with clients. It's something he calls the "Financial consulting process." It starts with a discovery/introductory meeting where he spends an hour with clients learning about their situation, telling them about his own background and expertise, and, if necessary, offering some introductory financial education. A two-hour meeting follows. In this next confab, the client brings financial data and other documents and they continue to discuss issues of concern. At a third meeting, Albritton presents an action plan identifying challenges, telling his clients how to eliminate dangers and solve problems, answering questions and generally trying to help the client make smarter decisions. A fourth meeting follows, if necessary, to review the financial action plan, answer questions and make suggestions to implement the best strategies. Another meeting occurs 45 days later, to make sure the client is on track and executing the agreed-upon strategies. Finally, quarterly meetings take place. I outline this process in detail because it's unique. It's a high-touch approach that many investors want, but unfortunately, don't get.

$UMMARY $UCCESS $TRATEGY

TO CONQUER INVESTING MISTAKE# 26:

Check out your broker or financial planner's background. Get references, call NASD's Public Disclosure Information Center at 800-289-9999, and ask potential advisors for Parts 1 and 2 of their ADV Forms, which disclose their professional and regulatory history.

27
MISTAKE

FIRING A BROKER OR PLANNER WITHOUT GOOD CAUSE – OR NOT FIRING ONE WHEN NECESSARY

I sympathize with stockbrokers these days.

They're having a tough time, with the slide in the capital markets, layoffs happening industry-wide, and corporate mergers among financial services firms resulting in even more pink slips.

To top it all off, investors are getting more than a little testy with their brokers. In fact, many people with beaten down portfolios are second-guessing their stockbrokers and financial advisors.

More to the point, an increasing number of individual investors are sending their brokers packing because, in the customers' minds, they're getting inefficient service, a lack of value or substandard performance. Mind you, most investors aren't becoming pure do-it-yourselfers. Many investors used to think they could hold down a full-time job, look after the kids, visit the in-laws, handle the grocery shopping, attend the town council meeting, read the Sunday paper – *and* manage their investments alone. Those days are long gone. These days, even as investors are giving their brokers the ax, they're seeking out smarter, better advisors. Even if this means they have to pay more to get them.

If you are unsatisfied with your broker or financial planner, you may have entertained thoughts of canning him or her. But is that really necessary? If you're upset because your portfolio has gone done recently, that's hardly justification to send your advisor packing. Even if you focus on absolute returns, it's probably not realistic to demand portfolio gains every single year. It's also unreasonable to fire someone just because one or two recommendations they made didn't pan out.

TAKE A CUE FROM THE RICH

It's particularly noteworthy that well-to-do investors don't make a practice of hopping from one advisor to the next. In fact, many well-heeled investors typically stick with their advisors for long periods of time. A survey by Matthew Greenwald & Associates, the New York polling firm, found that nearly 90% of affluent individuals stay with their first financial advisor. Greenwald & Associates surveyed 805 people under the age of 60, with more than $150,000 in annual household income.

The Greenwald & Associates survey also asked what investors were seeking in a financial advisor. And even wealthy, presumably more sophisticated investors still want good old-fashioned financial education. The poll said 73% of those surveyed were looking for someone to teach them about financial planning.

TO FIRE OR NOT? – THAT IS THE QUESTION

With this information in mind, here are six reasons that you might go ahead and fire your broker or financial planner – along with some tips about when you shouldn't.

By the way, this information isn't just helpful for anyone who uses a financial intermediary to invest. It's also practical guidance for brokers, money managers and financial advisors who want to know how to retain clients – in up and down markets.

1) I Inherited My Broker

There's a saying that, in life, we can't choose our parents and family members. That's true. But it's certainly not the case for our brokers. Yet, hoards of investors remain locked in the uncomfortable position of having "inherited" a broker. In many cases, these investors feel no connection or have little, if any, rapport with their advisors.

Think about whether you "inherited" your broker. If so, it probably happened when you inherited some money from a family member or loved one. In the process, you inherited the broker who was managing those funds. Many adults also often default to using the brokers their parents used.

Others get assigned a "new" broker after their original broker quits to join another firm, leaves the industry, retires, or loses his job in a merger. Whatever the reason, it can make you a little squeamish to have to deal with a new or unfamiliar broker or financial planner. Does this mean you should let the person go?

Not necessarily. The key is to judge how well the broker attempts to address your needs. (Don't fall for someone just because he says: "Your grandfather was always very happy here.") Smart brokers know that the getting-to-know-you period can be an uneasy time. So it's wise for them to give these clients extra attention during this transition.

2) I lost HOW MUCH money?!?

Is there anything worse for an investor? You get your quarterly statement or a phone call from your broker telling you that a stock you were heavily invested in has crashed, leaving you with huge financial losses.

Do you scream at the broker? (Why not, you figure: it was

her recommendation in the first place). Well, you could throw a tantrum. But it probably wouldn't do you much good. Taking a beating in the stock market – or in any market for that matter – is always a painful thing. Nevertheless, it doesn't make sense to summarily dismiss your broker just because one or two investments didn't work out. Firing a broker or planner under these circumstances is especially foolish if you've enjoyed an otherwise satisfactory, long-term relationship.

Instead, view the "bad" recommendation in the context of all the other suggestions the advisor has made. On balance, have the "good" recommendations far outweighed the bad? If so, stay put.

But woe to the broker who is consistently giving his or her customers bad advice and touting stocks that only head south. "If you aren't making money and the broker is, that's the best reason to fire him or her," Judith Berkey once told me. She's an investor and part-time computer consultant who lives in the suburbs of Washington D.C.

Think about it this way: why would you *pay* someone money to *lose* more of your money? That's like continuing to shop at a department store that you know always stocks inferior merchandise and has lousy customer service.

One caveat, though, to investors: if you know you lack the time, skills or inclination to manage your own brokerage account, seek out a competent professional. Besides, "it's folly to think that individual investors, as a group can outperform professionals, as a group," says Leonard Weiss, head of Weiss Wealth Management in Birmingham, Mich. Weiss, an industry veteran of 25 years, says he spends 50 hours a week studying the market. Yet he doesn't hold himself out as an all-knowing stock-market guru.

When it comes to stock-picking, "I don't know if my next decision is going to be my best one or my worst one," admits Weiss. "But if you let me make 10 or 20 decisions, I don't think I'll fail you because the process is what makes me good, not me."

3) Buy, buy, buy – now!

Nothing irritates investors more than when stockbrokers and financial advisors only seem interested in pushing a product. That's what happened to Tukufu Zuberi, a sociology professor at the University of Pennsylvania in Philadelphia. He finally had to fire his broker after he realized "the only time she called was to pitch a stock and it was just overbearing."

In this day and age, brokers should be doing more than just trying to generate commissions. They must offer value-added service because "among banks, brokerages and insurance firms, everyone is competing for the same assets," says Frank Bianchi, head of American Management Systems, a Fairfax, Va. consulting firm that provides CRM, or customer relationship management, software and other services to the financial services industry.

4) That's simply not right

Any stockbroker, financial planner or advisor who does things that are not in the client's best interest should be fired. What are some examples? Making unauthorized trades, "churning" a customer's account by buying and selling securities just to get commissions, and so forth. Investors don't take these things lightly – and they shouldn't. A record number of people are accusing their brokers of improper dealings. Just look at arbitration claims being filed with the NASD, which handles 90% of all investment disputes between customers and brokers. Through June 2003, NASD new arbitration filings hit 4,654 cases, up 25% from the comparable period in 2002.

Many times, arbitration disputes involve complaints from investors who lost money, and now have a case of "sour grapes." Of course, there are plenty of instances where an investor does have a legitimate gripe, like when a broker puts the client's money into investments that are clearly unsuitable for the client, given his or her goals, risk tolerance, age, etc.

DON'T TOLERATE CROOKS

It almost goes without saying, but any financial advisor who does something illegal is courting the wrath of his or her clients — and possibly worse consequences. What's illegal? Stealing comes to mind. "Borrowing" money from one client's account temporarily to put those funds someplace else is another example of illegal activity.

When a dispute moves beyond a point of a misunderstanding – say you told your broker to sell $10,000 worth of shares, but he thought you said to sell 10,000 shares – and involves downright intentional dishonesty, you have a duty to take action.

Investors who let corrupt brokers off the hook are allowing themselves to get taken advantage of and, in some instances, ripped off. Unfortunately, investors who don't do anything about unscrupulous brokers feed into what is often a pattern of abuse. Because a broker gets away with misconduct, he repeats bad behavior with future customers. Consequently, an unknown number of unsuspecting investors get scammed.

Think about it this way: if your car was stolen, you'd certainly report it to the police, wouldn't you? By the same token, don't take any illegal shenanigans from a broker. Report a broker's illegal activity immediately to a branch manager. Inform regulators or consumer groups about misconduct by independent investment advisors. Document everything. Put your complaints in writing. You may need written support if you have to go to arbitration, Wall Street's dispute-resolution process.

I remember writing back in the 1990s about a woman name Janie Thomas. She was a high-powered stockbroker in Merrill Lynch's Las Vegas branch. Thomas billed herself as the "broker to the stars" and boasted that she had numerous celebrity clients – including actress/singer Barbra Streisand and singer Paul Anka. But authorities say Thomas was the real performer. She allegedly created phony offshore accounts and lied to people about how well their investments were doing. The 32-year-old Thomas eventually skipped town (with her husband in tow) and has never been found. But her clients didn't take their plight lying down. They complained – and got compensated by Merrill Lynch — to the tune of an estimated $16.5 million. To Merrill's credit, it made all the investors whole.

5) Same Advice, Different Client

Brokers who offer only boilerplate advice or give cookie-cutter suggestions aren't doing their jobs. Period. "People can get generic financial planning and asset allocation recommendations free off the Internet. So good financial advisors really need to offer people customized solutions," says Robert Wolfe, a CERTIFIED FINANCIAL PLANNER™ practitioner with Capital Planning Group in Fort Lauderdale, Fla. "To the extent that a broker or advisor isn't doing that, he or she should be replaced," Wolfe adds.

Getting personalized service and value-added products and information is a top concern for Gregory Beckstrom, an investor from Minneapolis. In early 2001, he decided that he "needed more expert assistance." So he closed his account with a discount brokerage and turned his sizeable portfolio over to a broker at full-service firm.

"A lot of us got our fingers burned" in 2000, says Beckstrom, a geologist at an engineering firm. He used to obsess over his investment holdings. But "now I sleep better at night," Beckstrom says, adding that his current asset allocation mix is tailor-made for his needs.

6) Promises, Promises

Another investor turnoff: brokers who raise clients' hopes of achieving unrealistic returns. What's unrealistic? Anytime an advisor tells you that a certain investment is "guaranteed" to appreciate, or that you can expect 25% annual returns in the stock market — even though historically stocks have risen by about 10% a year. Even if you have an advisor who talks about more reasonable returns, you should make a point of remembering those conversations — and later hold the broker accountable.

Tukufu Zuberi, the Philadelphia investor, practices this strategy. "Brokers usually try to promise you 10% to 15% annual returns," he said. "So now, when I meet with my advisors I bring the past year's (performance) report and I ask them why the target was or wasn't achieved."

In some cases, you may need to have your advisors lower those expected return figures — or show you how they'll make up a shortfall, a difficult task in today's market.

And don't be pacified by brokers who simply try to convince you that everything is fine because they're "monitoring" the situation. "Monitoring is good," Zuberi notes. "But that's not enough."

PARTING COMPANY

Remember: Individuals who stick with brokers that should be fired experience dissatisfaction with their mix of investments or the specific securities chosen. They get frustrated about the investing process. They obtain little, if any, value-added service. And they often feel that they've received bad counsel because they are saddled with lackluster or poor-performing investments.

Breaking up is always hard to do, but sometimes it's necessary to give your broker or planner the ax. If you do so, just make sure you have good cause. Also, if you do part company with your financial advisor, be sure to get all your financial documents. Before you make the split, ask for current statements from the banks and brokerage firms with which you're doing business.

$UMMARY $UCCESS $TRATEGY
TO CONQUER INVESTING MISTAKE# 27:

Keep a financial advisor who is working in your best interest – and fire one that isn't. Good advisors don't just push products. They try to understand your overall financial situation and your personal needs. They also actively work to help you reach your goals.

28
MISTAKE

BEING DISHONEST OR GIVING YOUR ADVISORS INCOMPLETE INFORMATION

When you go to the doctor for an annual physical exam, or complaining of a backache, what's the first thing you'll probably be asked to do? Chances are a nurse will say, to put it bluntly: "Strip."

In order for the doctor to properly evaluate you, you'll probably have to bare yourself a bit.

The same principle holds true when you deal with financial advisors. Yet, too many investors – especially high net worth clients – refuse to disrobe, so to speak, in from of their stockbrokers or financial planners. These investors keep their cards "close to the vest" and decline to reveal all kind of personal, yet very pertinent, information. In some cases, wealthy investors "forget" to tell one broker about another large account that is held at another brokerage firm. At other times, investors omit personal information, such as the fact that they've been laid off – and have been out of work for the past six months.

Without an accurate picture of an investor's financial situation, an advisor is likely to offer an inaccurate diagnosis of what steps or strategies can benefit the investor. This means the investor's holdings may fare worse than the overall market and carry more risk.

To avoid this pitfall, it's vital that you are truthful and thorough in giving your financial advisor information. And don't worry about them trying to make a buck off of you. Just because you tell them about other assets you own, doesn't mean they'll bother you about those accounts. Yes, it is possible that they may tell you about the benefits of "consolidating" those accounts – no doubt with their firm. But chances are, they won't make an issue of it. And remember, the truth of the matter is there is value in having fewer funds, because you have less paperwork to track and you may be able to pay lower fees with higher account balances.

But a primary reason that you need to be upfront with your advisors is because they are often making recommendations based largely on the information you give them. They might recommend certain stocks, bonds or other assets, not knowing that you already have those securities. Then you would suffer from "portfolio overlap" or a duplication of your investments. This situation could also very easily cause your asset allocation to be thrown off balance. The end result would be that your overall portfolio may not perform as well as expected.

ACCOUNT AGGREGATION

Some firms will also be able to offer you one of the most popular new services being offered by financial services firms: account aggregation. This is an online feature that allows you to have a snapshot view of all your money matters: assets, liabilities, credit card debts, investments, and even frequent flyer miles. Though consumer advocates say account aggregation raises privacy and security concerns, this service may be helpful for those with complicated, dynamic lives.

ENCOURAGE DIALOGUE AMONG YOUR ADVISORS

Bruce Schwenger, the CEO of Harris*direct*, an online brokerage, told me that his company is well aware that it typically has only about

20% of a client's assets. No matter, though. Schwenger's firm encourages a "team approach." Its financial specialists employ a collaborative strategy in working with an investor's other advisors, including insurance specialists, accountants, attorneys or other financial pros.

Some people mistakenly think that their CPA – who might only do their taxes right now – really has no need to know their other financial business. Nothing could be further from the truth. And besides, your CPA may just become your financial advisor in the future. According to American Institute of Certified Public Accountants (AICPA), about 66,000 CPAs are now, or are in the process of becoming, registered investment advisors. CPAs are getting away from their traditional roles in part because clients need assistance in several areas of financial planning. This is good news for you, because your CPA's background in taxes and accounting may well enhance his or her ability to service your financial needs.

HONESTY REALLY IS THE BEST POLICY

Didn't your mother (or someone with good sense) always say: "Honesty is the best policy?" That truism is valuable to you as an investor too. So be truthful. Disclose all assets you own, even if you don't intend to marshal those assets under one roof. Also, let advisors know about life-changing events, such as divorce, because this will impact your finances.

A big challenge for financial advisors is keeping up with changes in their clients' lives. If you don't tell your advisor that you've had a death in the family, lost your job, got a fabulous new position paying twice your previous salary, have gotten remarried, or had a child, etc., how would they know? (Well, OK. If you're a woman, and you came strolling into their office 8 months pregnant, hopefully they'd have a clue.). But you get my point. Most investors want their advisors to be conscientious and communicative. But you've got to do your fair share of communicating as well. The telephone rings both ways.

$UMMARY $UCCESS $TRATEGY
TO CONQUER INVESTING MISTAKE# 28:

Give your financial advisors honest and complete information. An advisor can't fully help you or give you the best possible recommendations if he or she is only privy to part of your overall financial picture.

TAKING AN ADVISOR'S RECOMMENDATIONS ON BLIND FAITH

Investors who accept their advisors' every word without question may end up buying investments not in keeping with their comfort level for risk. Because they fear offending or second-guessing their broker, these investors keep quiet about decisions made by the advisor with which they don't agree. The result: the investor suffers the financial repercussions of poor decisions, and they sometimes sell investments at the wrong time. Furthermore, by taking a "hands off" approach with their advisors, these investors aren't truly learning about or developing a real appreciation for the investing process.

> On June 4, 2003, the yield on the 10-year Treasury note fell to 3.29%, hitting its lowest level in 45 years. That same day the Dow topped 9,000 for the first time since August 2002. And technology stocks were on fire, with Motorola rising 5.5% in a single day, Sun Microsystems soaring 6.6%, and Applied Materials gaining 5.2%. Depending on if you were a stock or a bond investor, you might have gotten a call from your broker advising you to buy or sell some of

these securities. Would you have been comfortable with any of them? What would you have done?

If your advisor makes a buy or sell recommendation that is inconsistent with your investment strategy, question the merit of that recommendation. Ask the advisor why deviating from your pre-set strategy is prudent, necessary or justifiable. Get comfortable asking your advisors to explain the rationale behind their suggestions.

Healthcare patients often get a "second opinion" when their doctors diagnose illnesses or make medical recommendations. Sometimes you may also need to get a "second opinion."

The idea here isn't to arbitrarily second-guess everything your broker or financial planner recommends. On the contrary, the more you trust your advisor, and feel secure in the knowledge that he or she is working in your best interest, the less you'll feel compelled to doubt or question that person's advice.

What I'm suggesting for all investors, though, is that you not shy away from talking to your advisors about why they recommend certain investments. It's particularly important for you to have these discussions if you feel the investment is a little too risky for your taste, or if you don't understand the investment and why it would complement or bolster your investing objectives.

$UMMARY $UCCESS $TRATEGY
TO CONQUER INVESTING MISTAKE# 29:

Listen to your advisor's recommendations – but don't take every suggestion on blind faith. Remember: you are ultimately responsible for ensuring your financial well-being. If you don't understand why a suggestion is being made, ask questions.

30

MISTAKE

BEING AN ABSENTEE OR DIFFICULT CLIENT

Based on my decade of experience as a financial journalist, and having listened to literally more than 1,000 financial planners, stockbrokers and others tell me about the investors with whom they deal, I can safely say that there are generally three types of clients:

1) The "absentee" client

2) The "difficult" client – also known as the "pain in the butt" client; and

3) The "ideal" client

My goal in this chapter is to help you get into category number three. In this final chapter, I'll tell you about serious mistakes you may be making in dealing with your financial intermediary that can cost you in more ways than just money. I'll also tell you how to make sure that you're one of your advisor's favorite customers, the ones they also call "dream" clients.

WHAT YOUR ADVISOR WON'T TELL YOU

This is information that your stockbroker or financial advisor would probably never dream of telling you. (Well, actually they might *dream* about it, but they wouldn't dare actually *say* it). And can you really blame them for not wanting to offend you? On the other hand, I can candidly tell you this information because I'm a third party. So trust me when I clue you in on this stuff, and believe me when I say that if you take the following do's and don'ts to heart, you'll have much better, much more effective relationships with your financial advisors. That, in turn, will make you happier about your finances, more knowledgeable about investing, and it probably will improve your portfolio performance as well.

Let's start with a brief overview of the typical investors: the "absentee," "difficult" and "ideal" clients. Then I'll give you the do's and don'ts you should follow.

THE ABSENTEE CLIENT

As the name suggests, an "absentee" client is largely away from or out of contact with his or her advisors. If you're an "absentee" client you may think that you're doing your broker or financial planner a favor. After all, you don't place demands on your advisor's time. You don't call them on the phone to fret over the fact that the Dow fell 200 points or that another Enron-type scandal has been unearthed. You don't insist on many in-person meetings. In fact, you really don't insist on much service, attention, or hand-holding at all. You're so out of touch with your advisor, though, that you're pretty much off his or her radar screen. And that is a definite mistake.

Absentee clients may suffer from a lack of information or knowledge about where their finances really stand. Because they only deal with their advisor's once a year – if that often – they probably don't have their portfolios assessed or rebalanced as frequently as might be necessary. These individuals also don't get much value-added insights from their advisors – simply because the broker or planner never connects with them to lend their expertise.

THE DIFFICULT CLIENT

We've all encountered difficult people before. Depending on the situation, they can be rude, offensive, unreasonable to talk to, and sometimes out of control. Now imagine that personality type – and picture that the person has just lost $10,000 or $20,000. Their overbearing personality is likely to *really* kick into overdrive.

But some other investors who are difficult clients aren't nasty people to deal with. It's just that they're sometimes ultra-whiny or they make completely unreasonable demands on their advisors' time. This is the investor who calls his or her broker practically every day – sometimes two or three times a day. This same individual has probably had half a dozen one-hour meetings in his or her advisor's office, and then turned those meetings into three-hour marathons.

Still another type of difficult client second-guesses almost every single thing his or her advisor says or does. It's one thing to question advice or recommendations that you don't understand, as I suggest you do. But it's another thing to contradict your broker because of some gossip you heard on an Internet investing chat room. This type of client gives his advisors big-time headaches. They sometimes cringe when they take your phone calls. They often dread talking to you, or meeting in person, simply because they know your patterns and unrealistic expectations. To top it all off, the difficult client who monopolizes an advisor's time will get haughty – or downright upset – if the advisor dares to try to bill the investor for that excessive time.

THE IDEAL CLIENT

Unlike the absentee client, and the difficult client, the ideal client knows how to strike the proper tone, balance and philosophy in dealing with his or her advisors. This individual is fully engaged in the process of investing and communicates clearly, concisely and regularly with financial advisors. To the advisor, an ideal client is neither incognito, nor ever-present. This person is, nonetheless, consistently on the advisor's mind. When you are an "ideal" or "dream" client, your advisor will think of you when reading an article or something of interest and send it to you. The advisor will call you up to see how you're doing and if you feel comfortable and on track with your financial goals.

The ideal client knows how to get his or her questions answered, stay in touch on a reasonable basis with financial advisors, and maintain a pleasant attitude during the process. As a result, the ideal clients' advisors *want* to work with them. Advisors want to further educate ideal clients financially. They take special pleasure in seeing those clients' money grow. And advisors especially enjoy witnessing an "ideal" client reach his or her goals.

In some cases, advisors may relish it when "difficult" clients meet their goals too. But in these instances, it's more likely that the advisor is feeling a sense of relief: "Whew!" he's thinking. "Now this person won't bug me as much!"

What I'm telling you here is not rocket science. And it's not that financial advisors don't want to talk to, interact with and help *all* their clients. Believe me, they do. But it's human nature to *especially* want to help those people you *like*.

I have had many, many advisors tell me, flat out, that when they are initially being interviewed by prospective clients, the "interview process" is really going both ways. Advisors are sizing you up, just as much as you are evaluating them. Advisors try not to take on investors that they personally don't like. Don't you do the same thing when you're seeking out business relationships?

So as an individual client, what can and should you do to get "most favored investor" status with your financial advisors?

Here are a few don'ts:

- **Don't call your advisor only to whine about one portfolio statement.** Focus on absolute returns. If you did, you wouldn't want to bite off your planner or broker's head if that one fund he recommended dropped by 7% but your overall portfolio is up 11%.

- **Don't focus on the negative.** When you call and say "did you hear that the Nasdaq is off 100 points?" you make your advisor think that you've not learned what proper investing is about. You're focusing on short-term, negative events and in all likelihood your planner is trying to get you to think about your long-term strategy. As a minor aside, the question, "Did you hear about the Nasdaq?" is also somewhat irritating and insulting. Of course they know! They follow the markets just as well as you do, if not better.

- **Don't second-guess your advisor unnecessarily.** Please try not to run to your financial planner asking: "Why don't I own XYZ stock?" just because you heard some Wall Street guru talking about it on television or radio. Whatever that person was recommending probably doesn't fit your personal situation.

- **Don't make unreasonable demands on your advisor's time.** Limit phone calls to what's necessary. Don't call too frequently or stay on the phone for an inordinate amount of time. Book face-to-face appointments when you think you need them, and resist the urge to "pop by" their office unexpectedly or unannounced. That's highly inconsiderate. Like you, your advisor has a million things to do. He or she could also be occupied with other clients in the office.

- **Don't let yourself be forgotten.** If your advisor has numerous clients, it's all too easy to slip into the ranks of being an "absentee" client. Stay in touch with periodic phone calls, and update your advisor if there are any big changes in your life that could affect your financial goals and needs.

Here are some do's you'd be wise to practice:

- **Do say "thank you."** You'd be surprised how far a simple verbal expression of gratitude, or even better a handwritten thank you note, can go. Your advisor will remember your thoughtfulness and you will stand out in his or her mind, because so few clients take the time to show their appreciation.

- **Do follow through on your advisor's recommendations.** It's frustrating for advisors when you sit in their office, nod your head in agreement with a plan of action they suggest, then fail to take any action.

- **Do come prepared for meetings.** If you've been asked to bring documents, come with a list of financial goals or whatever, keep your end of the bargain. Don't waste your advisor's time with meetings you're not ready to have.

- **Do be willing to pay for what you get.** Many investors want stop-everything-now service from their advisors, outstanding research, tailor-made investment products, and so forth. But they're not willing to pay for these things. That's not reasonable.

- **Do become a client who is liked and whose calls are enjoyed.** Remember, you're dealing with another human being. And chances are you'd get a lot better everything – better advice, better quality of information, more hand-holding if necessary, etc. – simply by being nice. A tip: send a holiday or birthday card. If you've got good advisors, let them know that they are valued and appreciated.

And just because there are plenty of financial planners out there – at last count more than 250,000 people identified themselves as financial planners – don't think you can treat your financial advisors as if they're a dime a dozen. Listen to the following advice from an investor who's found out how crucial it is to have the right financial advisor.

IN THEIR OWN WORDS: INVESTORS SHARE LESSONS LEARNED

My entire investing career has been one mistake after another. This is a result of not working with a good advisor. In the past 15 years, I have worked with seven investment counselors. I didn't realize how important it was to work with someone who understood and took the time to communicate. There were years when I did not speak to my advisor. I was a small potato and not very active, and I accepted that there was no reason for me to have a conversation with my agent.

In October of 1987, like most Americans, I lost money. I was scared and because I did not have a good relationship with my agent, I locked in my loss of $7,000. I stayed away from the market for years. I thought my next two advisors would be good because I knew them personally though my work in the community and my church. Another mistake. This did not guarantee that they had my best interest in mind. The fellow from my church, after he got my money locked into a plan which once again lost money, wouldn't even answer a question when I saw him in church.

I think what helped me turn the corner was finding a great accountant. After working with this gentleman for a couple of years, I went to him for advice about a new agent. He recommended a wonderful man who treats me like I'm important no matter how much money I have. He works well with both me and my husband. I even recommended him to an older friend of mine. She is now able to sleep at night without fear. I will probably be with my current advisor until death do us part. I feel confident and on track for the first time ever.

Getting the right person should not be taken lightly. Not only must they know their stuff, but they must have a great amount of emotional intelligence, sensitivity and communication skills.

Veronica Holcomb

Owner, VJ Holcomb & Associates

Like in all industries, it takes time and perseverance to find someone who is skilled and expert in the subject matters in which you need help – whether it's taxes, insurance, investment planning or whatever. Furthermore, there's no guarantee that the most qualified or knowledgeable person you find will click with you, or will want your business. It may not be anything personal, but that person could already be swamped with new clients or existing ones for that matter. One point of information, though, is that an abundance of fresh talent is constantly entering the field. The Bureau of Labor Statistics forecasts 40% growth in the financial planning profession between 1998 and the year 2008.

$UMMARY $UCCESS $TRATEGY
TO CONQUER INVESTING MISTAKE# 30:

Strive to become an "ideal" client who is engaged in the process of investing, but not over-bearing. Don't be a pesky "difficult" client who is a nuisance to financial advisors. But neither should you be an "absentee" investor who is readily forgotten.

I hope the information in this and all the other chapters proved valuable and eye-opening to you. I'm confident that if you conquer these 30 costly investing mistakes, you will definitely multiply your wealth!

Mistakes are a natural part of life. We all make mistakes: from goofs on the job to saying or doing the wrong things concerning our family members and friends. So it's unreasonable to assume that investing will be any different. Investing mistakes will inevitably occur. Nevertheless, I've often seen how difficult it is for people to talk about and admit their investing mishaps. Indeed, some people would sooner reveal very personal flaws or moral errors in judgment, rather than admit than their lack of investing prowess. It is my aim to help reduce the shame, guilt and embarrassment that many people feel about having made investing mistakes. Furthermore, I hope that by reading this book you will be informed, empowered and inspired to act.

I would love to hear about your investing successes or how you were able to correct any investing mistakes.

If you have a story you'd like to share, write to me personally at lynnette@InvestingSuccess.net.

I'm also collecting tales from investors who are courageous enough to admit their past shortcomings, and explain what they learned from those mistakes. Look at the front of this book for future titles planned in the *Investing Success*™ series. Then write and let me know if you happen to fit into any of those groups.

**If you'd like to be included in an upcoming
Investing Success™ book, send your tale to
mystory@InvestingSuccess.net.**

Your knowledge and experience could help other investors avoid the pitfalls you've encountered. And if your story is selected to be included in an upcoming *Investing Success*™ title, you'll get a free, autographed copy of the book.

I look forward to hearing from you.

NASAA - CSA INVESTMENT FRAUD AWARENESS QUIZ

The North American Securities Administrators Association (NASAA) is a membership organization of the 66 state, provincial and territorial securities administrators in the 50 states, the District of Columbia, Canada, Mexico, and Puerto Rico. In the United States, NASAA is the voice of the 50 state securities agencies responsible for grass-roots investor protection and efficient capital formation. The Canadian Securities Administrators (CSA) is the umbrella organization representing the 13 provincial and territorial securities commissions.

1. Which of the following phrases should raise your concern about an investment?

a. High rate of return

b. Risk-free

c. Your investment is guaranteed against loss

d. You must invest now

e. All of the above

2. Securities laws protect investors by requiring companies to:

a. Show profits before they can sell stock

b. Provide investors with specific information about the company

c. Pay dividends

d. Repay investors who have lost money

3. In which situation are you taking the least amount of risk?

a. Buying a Certificate of Deposit (CD), in United States, or a Guaranteed Investment Certificate (GIC), in Canada, from a bank

b. Investing with someone you know through your church or community association

c. Investing offshore

d. Investing with someone who contacted you by phone

4. A fellow book club member tells you about an investment opportunity that has earned returns of 20% during the past year. Your investments have been performing poorly and you're interested in earning higher returns. This person is your friend and you trust them. What should you do?

a. Ask your friend for more information about the investment so that you can understand the risks before you make a decision

b. Invest only a small amount to see how things go before making a larger investment

c. Call your securities regulator to see if the investment has been registered or is properly exempted for sale

d. a and c

5. Which of the following should you rely upon when making an investment decision?

a. Testimonials of other investors

b. Advertisements and news stories in the media or on the Internet

c. Technical data that you don't really understand

d. Information filed with your securities regulator

6. Ways to protect yourself from investment fraud include:

a. Read all disclosure documents about an investment

b. Seek advice from an independent and objective source

c. Be skeptical and ask questions

d. Never write the check/cheque for an investment in the name of your salesperson

e. All of the above

7. When dealing with a securities salesperson who is considered reputable, you should do all the following except:

a. Request copies of opening account documentation to verify that your investment goals and objectives are stated correctly

b. Open and review all correspondence and account statements when you receive them

c. Verify your written account statements with information you can obtain online

d. Allow the salesperson to manage your assets as they see fit because they are the expert

e. Evaluate your salesperson's recommendations by doing your own independent research

8. Which of the following are frequently used to defraud the public?

a. Short-term promissory notes

b. Prime bank investments

c. Offshore investments to avoid taxes

d. Nigerian advance fee letters

e. All of the above

9. The role of government securities regulators is to:

a. Sell shares to investors

b. Act as an association for securities dealers and advisers

c. Regulate securities markets, the investment industry and protect investors

d. All of the above

10. You have been working closely with your securities salesperson for years. Recently your salesperson asked you to invest in a product that he/she is really excited about, however, the recommendation seems very different from financial products you have invested in previously. Which of the following should you do?

a. Agree to make the investment because you have done business with your salesperson for years and trust them implicitly

b. Check with your securities regulator to see if they have any information on the investment product

c. Check with your securities regulator to see if the securities salesperson is authorized to sell the product in question

d. Rely upon the written material the salesperson gives you

e. a & d only

f. b & c only

11. An investment is likely to be legitimate if:

a. The promotional materials and company website look professional

b. The company has a prestigious office location

c. Other investors are receiving quick up-front returns

d. The company has an official-sounding name

e. None of the above

12. Who insures you against investment losses?

a. No one; this is the risk you take when you invest

b. My securities regulator

c. The company selling the investment

d. The Securities Investor Protection Corporation (SIPC) in United States or the Canadian Investor Protection Fund (CIPF) in Canada

Answers

1. Answer: e
Unusually high rates of return should be viewed as a cause for concern about an investment and would indicate a high-risk investment. Investigate all risk-free promises. Guarantees should also raise concern. Legitimate investments are not guaranteed against loss. Suggesting that you must invest "now" is generally

a high-pressure tactic used by swindlers to get the money before investors can change their minds or obtain more information.

2. Answer: b
Securities regulation is based on a disclosure system - laws requiring companies to provide investors with specific information. This ensures that investors have access to the information they need in order to make sound investment decisions. Companies do not have to show profits nor pay dividends in order to sell stock to investors. Also, companies are not required to repay investors who have lost money by investing in their shares.

3. Answer: a
Buying a CD or GIC is low risk, but you should investigate insurance levels in the event of the bank's failure. You should also consider inflation risk when dealing with low return investments. If you are going to invest with someone you know through your church or community association, you should ensure that both the person and the investment are properly registered/licensed with your securities regulator. You should thoroughly investigate **before** investing your hard-earned money. Investing offshore is not a guarantee of tax benefits. In addition, when you invest offshore, you are giving up some of the protections provided by your securities regulator. Investing with someone who calls you with an investment opportunity is also very risky. You should always be skeptical of telephone pitches.

4. Answer: d
You should never make an investment based simply on word-of-mouth, even if the recommendation comes from a family member, friend or acquaintance. Fraudulent schemes are frequently perpetuated this way. The promise of quick, high returns should also alert you to a possible scam. As a general rule, risk and return are proportional; the higher the return, the higher the risk. Even if a company looks and sounds legitimate, you should always check it out. Therefore, ask for more information about the investment and call your securities regulator to see if the investment has been registered or exempted for sale.

5. Answer: d

Information filed on an investment with your securities regulator can include disclosure documents, such as a prospectus or offering memorandum, and is meant to provide you with valuable information in order for you to make a wise investment decision. This is your best source of information about the history of the company and the risks associated with the investment. When shopping for investments, you should base your decisions on your own financial situation. If you don't understand an investment or if it feels too risky, don't invest in it.

News stories may be factual, but may not provide investors with enough information on which to base an investment decision. Ads are not necessarily factual. Be aware that con artists use advertisements, technical language, fake testimonials, and news stories to make their schemes appear legitimate.

6. Answer: e

Before making an investment, do your research and ensure that you understand what you are buying, the risks involved and if it is suitable for your personal financial situation. You can obtain written materials from your salesperson, go to the library, use the Internet, and/or get an opinion from another professional. Contact your securities regulator to ask about the salesperson's background and to verify proper licensing or registration of the investment and salesperson. Never transfer money in the name of a salesperson. Your check/cheque or fund transfer should always be directed to the company in which you are investing or to your brokerage/investment firm to settle your account.

7. Answer: d

Registered/licensed securities salespeople and their administrative staff can and do make errors. These errors and mistakes can be costly and need to be caught and corrected as soon as possible. More importantly, there have been instances where salespeople have intentionally abused their clients' trust through excessive trading in their accounts, selling them inappropriate financial products and outright fraud. Generally speaking, your salesperson should never buy or sell a security without first getting your approval.

8. Answer: e
With the presence of con artists and the ever-increasing complexity of financial products and markets, today's investors need to be well informed. The abovementioned items are all "scams" but represent only a small number of fraudulent investments that are currently being sold to unwitting investors. NASAA provides a current list of these scams that you can review at *www.nasaa.org*. Consumers need to maintain a heightened sense of caution when investing. Additionally, if the investment is something you are not familiar with, be sure to gather information and understand the product **prior to investing.** Consult with your securities regulator and review its website for additional investor education materials and information on scams.

9. Answer: c
Securities regulators administer the laws in their jurisdiction. One of their key mandates is to protect investors by ensuring that the rules and regulations are followed. Securities regulators do not sell shares directly to the public, but oversee the companies that do. They do not represent the industry, but provide protection to investors through rules, regulations and educational programs.

10. Answer: f
It is important to ask for and obtain written details of the investment recommendations you receive **before you make any decisions.** This could include a prospectus, an offering memorandum, research reports and other information. You should also contact your securities regulators for information relating to the registration or exemption status of the securities product in addition to checking to see if your salesperson is registered/ licensed to sell the investment product. You should **always** assess your investment objectives before making an investment in this, or any other product, to determine the risks involved, even if the recommendation comes from someone that you have done business with for many years.

11. Answer: e

You should not judge the legitimacy of an investment by the following: the look of the written promotional materials you receive; where the company's office is located; its website whether other investors received quick up-front returns; or the name of the company. All of these things may be done to lure investors into a scheme. Do your homework. Obtain information about the company from reputable sources such as the SEDAR website for Canadian publicly traded companies (*www.sedar.com*) or the EDGAR website for U.S. public securities filings (*www.sec.gov/edgar.html*) and call your securities regulator **before** you invest.

12. Answer: a

Any investment involves some degree of risk. You should know what degree of risk you are willing to take in order to meet your financial goals and objectives. Securities regulators protect investors by ensuring that securities laws and rules are abided by, but they do not insure investments. Be aware that there have been many problems with companies that falsely inform investors that their investments are guaranteed or insured. SIPC (*www.sipc.com*) in United States, and CIPF (*www.cipf.ca*) in Canada, do not insure investments or cover declines in investment value or fraudulent sales. SIPC and CIPF provide coverage in limited circumstances and with set dollar limits in the event of insolvency of a member brokerage firm. Investigate **before** you invest since you alone are bearing the risk involved with your investments.

Author's Note: Investment Fraud Awareness Quiz reprinted with permission from NASAA

NOTES

www.ingramcontent.com/pod-product-compliance
Lightning Source LLC
Chambersburg PA
CBHW020159200326
41521CB00005BA/193